To Live and Live Again

Published and Copyrighted © by
Sichos In English
788 Eastern Parkway · Brooklyn, New York 11213
Tel. (718) 778-5436

ISBN 1-8814-0018-2

5756 · 1995

תחיית המתים

ובאור תורת חסידות חב"ד

To Live a
Live Aga

An Overview of Techiyas Ha
Based on the Classical Sour
on the Teachings of Chabad Cl

by
Rabbi Nissan Dovid Dub

Edited by
Uri Kaploun

"You who repose in the d
Awaken and sing joyful pr
(Yeshay:

SICHOS IN ENGLISH
788 EASTERN PARKWAY
BROOKLYN, NEW YORK 11

5756 • 1995

TABLE OF CONTENTS

ב"ה

PUBLISHER'S FOREWORD

At some point very early in life, each of us becomes aware of how narrow the range of our vision inevitably is. Just as our mortal eyes cannot look further back than the day we were born, they cannot see further ahead than a certain other day in our physical lifetimes. Little wonder, then, that whenever we encounter a word about that uncharted future from the mouth of one of our Sages or Rebbeim, whose telescopic eyes (so to speak) have been shown its secrets, every such teaching is precious. Besides, for many Jews today, the Talmudic phrase *hilchesa diMeshicha* ("a law for the Days of *Mashiach*") no longer speaks of an era that is so far ahead that it becomes irrelevant and inconceivable: it speaks of an era that the Rebbe has assured us is just around the corner.

To Live and Live Again: An Overview of Techiyas HaMeisim Based on the Classical Sources and on the Teachings of Chabad Chassidism is a pioneering work. It was researched, written and annotated by Rabbi Nissan Dovid Dubov, emissary of *Chabad-Lubavitch* to the South London Jewish community, based at Chabad House, Wimbledon. Rabbi Dubov's research gleans from the *Tanach, Talmud, Midrash, Halachah, Kabbalah* and *Chassidus,* and echoes the underlying harmony of these seemingly diverse disciplines as repeatedly demonstrated in the published talks and letters of the Lubavitcher Rebbe.

The chapter headings of this work indicate its imposing scope, ranging from "The Purpose of Creation" to "Reincarnation," from "Life After the Resurrection" to "Who Will Rise?" The volume concludes with the full translated text of two related *maamarim* first delivered by the Rebbe: "To Understand the Concept of *Techiyas HaMeisim,* the Resurrection of the Dead," and "All Israel Have a Share in the World to Come."

To Live and Live Again was edited by Uri Kaploun, meticulously laid out and typeset by Yosef Yitzchok Turner, its cover was designed by Avrohom Weg, and it was coordinated through all its stages of publication by the Director of Sichos In English, Rabbi Yonah Avtzon.

Sichos In English

Rosh Chodesh Kislev, 5756 [1995]

AUTHOR'S PREFACE

The thirteenth Principle of Faith enumerated by Maimonides is belief in *Techiyas HaMeisim,* the Resurrection of the Dead. Resurrection figures frequently in our daily prayers and is echoed in many of our daily customs.

Though Rabbinic literature abounds with references to this subject, few are aware of its details. Certainly for the English reader, many of the primary sources are not easily accessible. Hence the present work, an overview which ranges from the Scriptures to contemporary Rabbinic writings, and is based primarily on the published talks and letters of the Lubavitcher Rebbe, Rabbi Menachem M. Schneerson.*

The writing of this book forms part of the worldwide program of study about the Messianic era and thereafter, initiated by the Rebbe. It is the hope of the author that through the publication of this and similar works, we will all merit the coming of *Mashiach* and the Resurrection speedily in our own days.

I would like to close with a warm word of gratitude to Rabbi Yonah Avtzon, Uri Kaploun and Yosef Yitzchok Turner of Sichos In English for their loving attention to every detail, and to my wife for her constant support and encouragement in our joint *shlichus.*

Rabbi Nissan Dovid Dubov
Wimbledon, U.K.

Rosh Chodesh Kislev, 5756 [1995]

---

* A responsum by the Rebbe on the Resurrection was originally published in *Kovetz Lubavitch,* then in *Teshuvos U'Biurim,* and later in the Rebbe's *Igros Kodesh* (Letters), Vol. I, p. 141ff.

Chapter 1

The Belief

"I believe with perfect faith that the dead will be brought back to life when G-d wills it to happen."[1]

RAMBAM'S DEFINITION

In his *Discourse on the Resurrection*,[2] *Rambam* writes: *"The concept of Resurrection* — which is well known among our people and accepted throughout all its circles, and which is often mentioned in the prayers and aggadic teachings and supplications (written by the prophets and the foremost Sages) with which the *Talmud* and the *Midrashim* are replete — *sig-*

---

1. This is the 13th and last of *Rambam's* Principles of Faith, in the paraphrased form that many *Siddurim* append to the morning prayers. (In their original form, the Principles appear in the *Rambam's* introduction to his Commentary on the *Mishnah* of *Sanhedrin*, ch. 10.) See also *Maimonides' Principles* by Rabbi Aryeh Kaplan (N.C.S.Y.).

2. *Maamar Techiyas HaMeisim*, (also known as *Iggeres Techiyas HaMeisim* — *Letter on the Resurrection*), beginning of ch. 4.

nifies the following: The soul will return to the body after they have been separated [by death]. No Jew has disputed this concept, and it cannot be interpreted other than literally. One may not accept the view of any Jew who believes otherwise.

"As I shall explain in the present discourse: Why should we not interpret these verses [regarding the Resurrection] allegorically, as we have done with many other Biblical verses, departing from their literal meaning? The reason is as follows: The concept of Resurrection, namely, that the soul will return to the body after death, is expressed by Daniel[3] in such a manner that it cannot be interpreted other than literally: 'Many of those who sleep in the dust of the earth shall awaken, some to everlasting life, and some to reproach and everlasting contempt.' Daniel was likewise told by the angel,[4] 'Now go your way to the end and rest, and you shall arise to your destiny at the end of days.'"

The *Talmud*[5] teaches that those who deny Resurrection will have no share in the World to Come, and *Rambam* in *Mishneh Torah*[6] rules that this teaching has the authority of *Halachah*.

SELECTIONS FROM THE TALMUD

[R. Elazar HaKapar[7]] used to say: "Those who are born are destined to die; those who are dead are destined to live again" *(another version:* 'to be resurrected').*"

* * *

---

3. *Daniel* 12:2.
4. *Ibid.*, v. 13.
5. *Sanhedrin* 90a.
6. *Hilchos Teshuvah* 3:6.
7. *Avos* ("Ethics of the Fathers") 4:22.

All[8] Israel have a share in the World to Come....[9] The following, however, have no share therein: He who maintains that Resurrection is not a Biblical doctrine....[10]

*   *   *

How[11] is Resurrection deduced from the Torah?[12]

---

8.   *Sanhedrin* 90a, in the *mishnah.*

9.   See at length in ch. 5 and in Appendix 2 (below). See also *Rashi* on the above-quoted *mishnah. Midrash Shmuel* on *Avos* understands *Rashi* to mean — and *Bartenura* holds likewise — that although the previous chapter of *Sanhedrin* referred to those liable for capital punishment, they too have a share in the World to Come.

In the Hebrew text, the literal translation of the above-quoted phrase is not "*in* the World to Come" but "*to* the World to Come" (לעולם הבא). See *Margaliyos HaYam*, citing *Ruach Chaim*, for an explanation of this observation and others.

The phrase "*to* the World to Come" calls to mind a teaching of the Rebbe Rayatz on the following phrase from the *Mishnah (Berachos* 1:5)* that is quoted in the *Haggadah:* כל ימי חייך: להביא לימות המשיח — "The phrase '*All* the days of your life' includes (lit., 'is to bring') the Messianic Era." The plain meaning of this phrase is that the Exodus is to be recalled not only during the days of our present life, but even in the days of the Messianic Era. Noting the literal meaning of the verb *lehavi* ("to bring"), the Rebbe Rayatz perceived an additional teaching in these words: Throughout all the days of your life, your *avodah* should be directed to bringing about the days of *Mashiach.*

Along these lines, in the phrase "All Israel have a share *to* the World to Come" one may perhaps find a hint that every Jew should play an active role in hastening the advent of the World to Come.

10. *Rashi* comments: "I.e., he denies the validity of the Scriptural interpretations — at the [non-literal] level of *derush* — through which the *Gemara* below proceeds to derive Scriptural authority for the concept of Resurrection. Even if he concedes and believes that the dead will be resurrected, but denies that this belief is alluded to in the Torah, he is a heretic *(kofer).* Since he denies its Biblical source, of what value to us is his faith? From where does he know that this is the case? Accordingly, he is unequivocally considered a heretic."

The author of *Beer Sheva* states that the above thought is originally quoted in *Yad Ramah* (יד רמ״ה) in the name of Rabbeinu Shlomo. See also the *Responsa* of *Rashba,* sec. 9.

It is written,[13] "Of [these tithes] you shall give G-d's heave-offering to Aharon the priest." But would Aharon live forever?! After all, he did not enter the Land of Israel and thereby make it possible that *terumah* be given to him! Rather, this verse teaches that he will ultimately be resurrected, and the Jewish people will give him *terumah*....[14]

*   *   *

R. Simai[11] says: "Whence do we learn Resurrection from the Torah? — From the verse,[15] 'And I also have established My covenant with them (i.e., the Patriarchs) to give them the Land of Canaan.' The verse does not say 'to give *you*' but 'to give *them*.' [Since, as *Rashi* points out, the Land was given to their descendants, and has not yet been given to them personally,] their future Resurrection is thus proved from the Torah."

*   *   *

Sectarians[11] asked Rabban Gamliel: "From where do we know that the Holy One, blessed be He, will resurrect the dead?"

He answered them from the Torah, the Prophets and the Hagiographa....

*   *   *

---

11.   *Sanhedrin* 90b.
12.   In the expositions that follow, the word "Torah" sometimes embraces the entire *Tanach*. See at length in *Margaliyos HaYam* on *Sanhedrin* 92a, sec. 3.
13.   *Bamidbar* 18:28.
14.   See ch. 11 below.
15.   *Shmos* 6:4. See *Maharsha* and *Rif* on *Ein Yaakov*.
      The *Gemara* in *Sanhedrin* 90b quotes a similar verse *(Devarim* 11:21, which is read in the course of the daily *Shema)* as part of Rabban Gamliel's response to the heretics. *Ben Yehoyada* (on *Sanhedrin, loc. cit.*) discusses why Rabban Gamliel did not instead refer his disputants to the earlier verse in *Shmos*.

Queen[11] Cleopatra said to R. Meir: "I know that the dead will live again, for it is written,[16] 'And they shall blossom out of the city like grass from the earth';[17] but when they arise, will they arise naked or clothed?"

He replied, "You may deduce the answer by observing a wheat grain.[18] If a grain of wheat, which is buried naked, sprouts forth in many robes, how much more so the righteous, who are buried in their garments."

An[11] emperor said to Rabban Gamliel: "You maintain that the dead will live again; but they turn to dust — and can dust come to life?!"

Thereupon the [emperor's] daughter[19] said to [Rabban Gamliel]: "Here, let me answer him. In our town there are two potters: one fashions his vessels from water, and the other from clay. Who is the more praiseworthy?"

"He who fashions them from water," replied [her father].

---

16. *Tehillim* 72:16.

17. Citing *Kesubbos* 111a, *Rashi* teaches that the righteous will pass through subterranean tunnels and be resurrected in Jerusalem. See ch. 7 below.

18. The *Gemara* often draws analogies with the wheat grain. (In *Kesubbos* 111b the *Gemara* cites the same answer in the name of R. Chiya bar Yosef.) *Ben Yehoyada* (on *Sanhedrin* 91a) points out that arguments of this kind are intended merely to provide additional support for beliefs which are based on Biblical verses. He aptly quotes the verse *(Devarim* 8:3), "Man does not live by bread alone: man lives on that which comes forth from G-d's mouth," and concludes: Ultimately, our faith is not nourished by arguments based on a grain of wheat, but by the words that come forth from G-d's mouth.

19. Why did she interject? *Ben Yehoyada* explains that since she was afraid that Rabban Gamliel might say that gentiles would not be resurrected, she offered her own inoffensive answer. He goes on to explain that the emperor in fact believed in G-d, but he was perplexed by the concept of Resurrection, for it appeared to defy the principle that "there is nothing new under the sun" *(Koheles* 1:9). Hence his daughter's answer: any process which already exists may be a prototype for Resurrection.

She concluded: "If He can fashion man from water,[20] surely he can do so from clay."[21]

* * *

According[22] to the School of R. Yishmael, [in the above exchange the emperor's daughter answered her father with] a different analogy: If glassware, made by the breath of mere flesh and blood, can be reconstituted when shattered, then how much more so man, who was created by the breath of the Holy One, blessed be He.

* * *

A[22] sectarian challenged R. Ami: "You maintain that the dead will live again; but they turn to dust — and can dust come to life?!"

He replied, "Let me offer you a parable. A mortal king commanded his servants to build him great palaces in a place where there was neither water nor earth [for making bricks]. They went and built them. After some time they collapsed, so he commanded them to rebuild them in a place which did have water and earth, but they said, 'We cannot.' The king was indignant: 'If you could build in a place that had neither water nor earth, surely you can build in a place where there is!'"[23]

R. Ami concluded: "And if you do not believe [that G-d can form creatures from dust], go out to the field and you will see a certain mouse; today it is part flesh and part dust,[24] and

---

20. *Rashi:* "From a drop of semen which resembles water."

21. See *Likkutei Sichos,* Vol. XVIII, p. 247.

22. *Sanhedrin* 91a.

23. *Rashi* offers two alternative ways of understanding this parable: (a) If G-d can create man from a small drop which is almost intangible, surely He can create him from dust; (b) G-d created the entire universe out of chaos.

24. *Margaliyos HaYam* cites *Tiferes Yisrael* on *Chullin* 9:6 to the effect that such a mouse exists in Egypt.

yet by tomorrow it has become entirely flesh. And should you say that this metamorphosis takes a long time ['and hence argue that G-d does not revive the dead in an instant' — *Rashi*], go up to the mountain; there you will see but one snail, whilst after tomorrow's rain the mountain will be covered with snails ['which are generated immediately' — *Rashi*]."

* * *

A[22] sectarian said to Geviha ben Pesisa: "Woe to you, you wicked ones, who maintain that the dead will revive! The living indeed die, but shall the dead live?!"

He replied: "Woe to you, you wicked ones, who maintain the dead will not revive. If those who never lived, now live, surely those who have lived, will live again!"

* * *

Resh Lakish[25] contrasted two verses: "One verse promises,[26] 'I will gather them in...; among them there will be the blind and the lame, the woman with child together with the woman in labor.' Another verse, however, states:[27] "Then shall the lame man leap like a hart, and the tongue of the dumb shall sing, for waters shall break forth in the wilderness, and streams in the desert.' How so? — They shall rise with their defects[28] and then be healed."

* * *

Ulla[25] contrasted two verses: "It is written,[29] 'He will destroy death forever, and G-d will wipe away tears from all

---

25. *Sanhedrin* 91b.
26. *Yirmeyahu* 31:8.
27. *Yeshayahu* 35:6.
28. And thus be identifiable *(Bereishis Rabbah* 95:1) See also *Margaliyos HaYam*, and ch. 9 below.
29. *Yeshayahu* 25:8.

faces,' whilst elsewhere it is written,[30] 'For a child shall die a hundred years old....' However, this presents no difficulty: one verse refers to Jews, the other to heathens. But what business have heathens there? — The reference is to those of whom it is written,[31] 'And strangers shall stand and pasture your flocks, and the sons of the alien shall be your plowmen and your vine-dressers.'"[32]

* * *

Rava[25] also contrasted two quotations: "It is written,[33] 'I kill, and I make alive.' [Rashi: 'This implies that a man is resurrected in the same state (e.g., wounded) as he was at the time of death.'] The same verse goes on to say, 'I have wounded, and I heal!' [Rashi: 'This implies that a wounded man is resurrected whole.'] Yet there is no contradiction here, for in this verse the Holy One, blessed be He, is saying: 'What I kill I make alive' [i.e., in the same state], and 'What I have wounded, I then heal.'"[34]

* * *

On[25] the verse,[33] "I kill, and I make alive," our Sages commented: "One might understand this to mean, 'I kill one person and give life to another,' as is the way of the world, ['so that one man dies and another is born' — Rashi]. The same verse therefore goes on to say, 'I have wounded, and I heal.' Just as wounding and healing [obviously] refer to the same person, so putting to death and bringing to life refer to the same person. This is an answer to those who maintain that Resurrection is not intimated in the Torah."

* * *

---

30. *Ibid.* 65:20.
31. *Ibid.* 61:5.
32. See ch. 10 below.
33. *Devarim* 32:39.
34. *Rashi:* "As with the above teaching [of Resh Lakish]."

R. Meir[25] said: "From where do we learn Resurrection from the Torah? — From the verse,[35] אז ישיר משה ('Moshe and the Children of Israel then sang this song to G-d'). The literal meaning of the verb is not 'sang' but 'shall sing.' Thus *Techiyas HaMeisim* is taught in the Torah."[36]

* * *

R. Yehoshua ben Levi[25] said: "Where is Resurrection derived from the Torah? — From the verse,[37] אשרי יושבי ביתך, עוד יהללוך סלה ('Happy are those who dwell in Your house; they shall praise You forever'). The verse does not say, 'they praised You,' but 'they shall praise you.' Thus *Techiyas HaMeisim* is taught in the Torah.

* * *

R. Chiya bar Abba[25] said in the name of R. Yochanan: "Where in the Torah do we learn of Resurrection? — From the verse,[38] 'The voice of your watchmen is raised aloft: together shall they sing.' The verb ארננו does not mean 'sang' but 'shall sing'. Here, then, is a source in the Torah for *Techiyas HaMeisim*."

* * *

Rava[39] said: "Where is Resurrection derived from the Torah? — From the verse,[40] 'May Reuven live and not die.' [This seeming repetition implies:] 'May Reuven live *in this world,* and not die *in the next.*"

---

35. *Shmos* 15:1.
36. *Margaliyos HaYam* cites many sources for this teaching in the *Zohar*.
37. *Tehillim* 84:5.
38. *Yeshayahu* 52:8.
39. *Sanhedrin* 92a.
40. *Devarim* 33:6.

Ravina said it is derived from this verse:[3] "Many of those who sleep in the dust of the earth shall awaken, some to everlasting life, and some to reproach and everlasting contempt."[41]

R. Ashi said it is derived from this verse:[4] "Now go your way to the end and rest, and you shall arise to your destiny at the end of days."

*   *   *

R. Tavi[39] said in the name of R. Yoshia: "What do we learn from the following text?[42] 'There are three things that are never satisfied:... the grave and the womb....' How comes the grave next to the womb? — This juxtaposition teaches you that just as the womb takes in and gives forth again, so the grave takes in and will give forth again. Moreover, if the womb which takes in silently gives forth with loud noise [i.e., the crying of the infant], does it not stand to reason that the grave which takes in with a loud noise [i.e., the wailing of the mourners], will give forth [those who are revived] with a loud noise?[43] Here is an

---

41.   "The verse does not say '*all* who sleep...shall awaken,' because this... would include all of mankind, and G-d made this promise only to Israel; hence the verse says, '*Many* of those who sleep...shall awaken.' Moreover: the phrase, 'some to everlasting life, and some to reproach and everlasting contempt,' does not mean that among those who are resurrected some will be rewarded and some punished, for those who deserve punishment will not be resurrected at the time of the Redemption. Rather, it means that those who awaken will have everlasting life, and those who will not awaken will be destined to reproach and everlasting contempt. For all the righteous [including those] who repented, will live; only the unbelieving and those who died without repentance will remain. All this will happen at the time of the Redemption." — R. Saadiah Gaon, *Emunos VeDeos*, ch. 7.

   See also Ibn Ezra *(ad loc.)*; *Rambam, Peirush HaMishnah*, on *Sanhedrin*, ch. 10; *Ramban, Shaar HeGemul*, ch. 11; *Or HaShem*, Part 3, 4:4, p. 77. See, however, Abarbanel, *Maayanei HaYeshuah*, p. 11a.

42.   *Mishlei* 30:15, 16.

43.   *Rashi* cites the verse *(Yeshayahu* 27:13), "And it shall be on that day, that a great *Shofar* shall be sounded...." The *Midrash* entitled *Osios*

answer for those who deny that *Techiyas HaMeisim* is taught in the Torah."

* * *

Tanna dvei Eliyahu[39] states: "The righteous whom G-d will resurrect will not revert to dust, for it is said,[44] 'And it shall come to pass that he who is left in Zion and he who remains in Jerusalem shall be called holy: everyone in Jerusalem who is inscribed for life.' Just as the Holy One endures forever, so too shall they endure forever."

* * *

Three[45] keys have not been entrusted to an agent: the keys to birth, rain and Resurrection.[46]

* * *

R. Eleazar[47] said: "The illiterate will not be resurrected, for it is written,[48] 'The dead will not live...,' but since this might be assumed to refer to all, the verse goes on to say, 'The shades of the dead (רפאים) shall not rise,' thus alluding specifically to him who is lax (מרפה עצמו) in studying the words of the Torah."

> *deRabbi Akiva* elaborates (sec. 9): "How will the A-mighty resurrect the dead in the time to come? He will take up a *Shofar* a thousand cubits long and will sound it, and it will reverberate from one end of the world to another. With the first blast the world will be in an uproar; with the second, the earth will split," and so on. See also *Pirkei deRabbi Eliezer*, sec. 34.

44.   *Yeshayahu* 4:3.
45.   *Sanhedrin* 113a.
46.   Cf. the *mishnah* at the end of Tractate *Sotah*, "Resurrection comes through Eliyahu (the Prophet Elijah)." (According to *Emek HaMelech, Shaar Olam HaTohu*, sec. 29, this means that the key to the dew of Resurrection was entrusted to the hands of Eliyahu.) The *Jerusalem Talmud (Shekalim 3:3)* states, "Resurrection brings about [the coming of] Eliyahu." See the comment of *Ran* on *Avodah Zarah* 20b.
47.   *Kesubbos* 111b. See also *Tanna dvei Eliyahu*, sec. 5.
48.   *Yeshayahu* 26:14.

Said R. Yochanan to him: "It gives no satisfaction to their Master that you should speak of such people in this manner.[49] That text speaks of a man who was so lax as to worship idols!"

Replied [R. Elazar]: "Then let me base my exposition [to the same effect] on another text. It is written,[50] '[Your dead shall live, my dead body shall arise; awake and sing, you who repose in the dust.] For Your dew is a dew of light, and the earth shall cast down the shades of the dead.' This means that he who makes use of the light of the Torah, him will the light[51] of the Torah revive, but as to him who does not make use of the light of the Torah, him will the light of the Torah not revive."

Observing however, that [R. Yochanan] was [still] distressed, [R. Elazar] said to him: "Master, I have found a remedy for [the illiterate] in the Torah, for it is written,[52] 'But you who cleave to the L-rd your G-d are all alive today.' Now is it possible to *cleave* to the Divine Presence, concerning Whom it is written,[53] 'For the L-rd your G-d is a consuming fire'?! The meaning is this: Any man who marries his daughter to a scholar, invests on behalf of scholars, or benefits scholars from

---

49.   "G-d does not desire that you judge Israel so harshly" *(Rashi* on the same sentence in *Sanhedrin* 111a).

50.   *Yeshayahu* 26:19.

51.   A footnote in *Likkutei Sichos,* Vol. XI, p. 193, observes that *Yalkut Shimoni* on this verse writes that "the *dew* of the Torah will revive him"; so, too, *Tanya,* ch. 36. See also: *Jerusalem Talmud, Berachos* 5:2; *Shabbos* 88b; *Likkutei Torah, Parshas Haazinu,* p. 73c.

     The *maamar* entitled *Samchuni* (in *Sefer HaMaamarim 5660*) explains that *or Torah* ("the light of the Torah") signifies *razin* (the secrets of the Torah) while *tal Torah* ("the dew of the Torah") signifies *razin derazin* (the innermost secrets of the Torah).

52.   *Devarim* 4:4.

53.   *Ibid.,* v. 24.

his estate is regarded by the Torah as if he had cleaved to the Divine Presence."

*   *   *

R. Chiya bar Yosef[47] said: "A time will come when the righteous will break through the soil and rise up in Jerusalem, for it is written,[16] 'And they shall blossom out of the city like grass from the earth'[17] — and 'city' can allude only to Jerusalem, as in the phrase,[54] 'For I shall defend this city.'"

---

54.   *II Melachim* 19:34.

Chapter 2

The Purpose of Creation

"The purpose for which this world was created is that the Holy One, blessed be He, desired to have an abode in the lower worlds."[55]

WORLDS:
DIVINE
SELF-CONCEALMENT

Since the beginning of time, man has grappled with the question, "What is the purpose of Creation?" And, the greatest thinkers among our people have answered it in different ways.[56]

---

55. *Likkutei Amarim — Tanya,* ch. 36, paraphrasing *Midrash Tanchuma, Parshas Naso,* sec. 16.

56. The first discourse in *Sefer HaMaamarim 5666* by the Rebbe Rashab, R. Shalom Dovber of Lubavitch, discusses all the reasons for creation enumerated in the *Zohar* and *Etz Chaim,* and the various expositions of the above-quoted *Midrash.* See also *Likkutei Sichos,* Vol. VI, p. 18ff.

The exposition of R. Shneur Zalman of Liadi[57] — the first Lubavitcher Rebbe, known by chassidim as "the Alter Rebbe" — is based on the *Midrash* paraphrased above, that the purpose of creation is that G-d wished to have a *dirah betachtonim*,[58] a dwelling place in the lower worlds.

What is meant by "worlds"?[59]

G-d is infinite. He is perfection. Accordingly, His power extends not only throughout the realm of the infinite: He embraces both infinite and finite powers. And in order for Him to create this finite world, it was (so to speak) necessary for Him to conceal the infinite and reveal the finite.

A concealment of G-d's true essence is called a "world". This is reflected in the Holy Tongue, in which עולם *(olam —* "world"*)* shares a root with העלם *(he'elem —* "concealment"*)*.

The *Kabbalah* describes how G-d created the world not in one step, but rather in a gradated process called *Seder Hishtalshelus* — the chainlike scheme by which the creative Divine light undergoes successive stages of self-concealment in the course of its descent from G-d's ethereal transcendence to the creation of tangible physicality. Each successive link in the chain is a further concealment of the infinite, and a further revelation of the finite.

---

57. *Tanya*, chs. 36 and 37.
58. I.e., a home in the lowest of all worlds.
59. For a full discussion, see *Mystical Concepts in Chassidism*, by R. Jacob Immanuel Schochet, that is also appended to the bilingual edition of *Tanya*. See also *The Thirteen Petalled Rose*, by R. Adin Even-Yisrael (Steinsaltz).

THE
FOUR
WORLDS

In general terms, there are (in descending order) Four Worlds:

1. *Atzilus* — the World of Emanation;

2. *Beriah* — the World of Creation;

3. *Yetzirah* — the World of Formation;

4. *Asiyah* — the World of Action.

These Worlds correspond to the four letters of the Tetra-grammaton, the Divine Name: the letter *yud* corresponds to the World of *Atzilus,* the upper letter *hei* corresponds to *Beriah,* the letter *vav* to *Yetzirah,* and the lower letter *hei* to *Asiyah.*

The greatest degree of Divine self-concealment, i.e., the lowest of the worlds, is *Asiyah,* the World of Action. This is where "our world" and "we" are. In this world G-d has concealed His Presence so severely and so efficiently, that it is possible for people here to actually (heaven forfend) deny His existence.

It is only in such a world, where only the trained eye will perceive the Creator, that free choice may be given to man; hence it is only in such a world that reward and punishment are warranted. In the "higher" worlds, by contrast, G-d's Presence is so indisputably manifest that the angels who inhabit the Worlds of *Beriah* and *Yetzirah* have no free choice. Indeed, so directly do they experience G-d's Presence that they stand continually in a state of awe.

This was G-d's will — that there also be created a world whose creatures could not see G-d. Accordingly, he did not endow the physical eye with the capability to see Him. Only with the mind's eye can the Divine be apprehended, and this is made possible by G-d's self-revelation. For example, when G-d gave our people the Torah, the blueprint of Creation, He is described as having "come down" on Mt. Sinai. Since He is everywhere, this phrase is merely a metaphor for revelation.[60]

The revelation of the infinite light of G-d's Essence radiates in any of ten modes. The first of these ten emanating Divine attributes or *Sefiros* is called *Chochmah* (lit., "wisdom"). This wisdom is embodied in the Torah,[61] and just as G-d existed before the world was created, so too did His wisdom then exist. Indeed, to quote the metaphor of the *Zohar*,[62] G-d "looked into the Torah and created the world," rather like a builder looking into the architect's plans.

THE
TASK OF
MANKIND

Having hidden Himself in this world, G-d then entrusted man with the task of revealing its true essence, and transforming its darkness into light — transforming the world's superficial obscurity into an environment in which G-d's Presence is felt, and in which He feels (so to speak) at home.

For mankind at large, this task entails the observance of the Seven Noachide Laws[63] that provide any society with civilized foundations; for Jews, this task entails the observance of the 613 commandments of the Torah. In the Holy Tongue, the word meaning "commandment" (מצוה — *mitzvah*) shares a root with the Aramaic word for "connection" (צותא — *tzavsa*). In other words, the observance of each particular *mitzvah* has its own distinctive way of connecting the individual with the Giver

---

60.   See *Targum* on *Shmos* 19:20.
61.   See *Tanya*, chs. 3, 23.
62.   *Zohar* I, 134a.
63.   In the original, *sheva mitzvos bnei Noach.*

of the commandments. By setting up all 613 connections with G-d,[64] we reveal His Presence on earth; we fashion the dwelling place, the *dirah betachtonim,* that He desired.

This explains why it is in this physical world, in the World of Action, that the commandments must be fulfilled, for their function is to refine and elevate the world. In our present circumstances, however, the physical world can be uplifted only to a certain degree. Not until the Messianic Era, and thereafter in the time of Resurrection, will all mankind be sufficiently sensitized to perceive G-d. At that time, when all creatures will know their Creator, His dwelling place will be complete. The ultimate purpose of creation is thus the Messianic Era and the period that follows it.

This revelation, however, depends on our actions and Divine service throughout the duration of the present *galus* ("exile").[65]

Our life in this exile is as unreal and as inconsistent as a dream. In a dream, one can envisage anomalies; one can see oneself walking on the ceiling. Likewise, in the present state of *galus,* we can know all about G-d, yet at the same time be occasionally oblivious to His commandments. Contrasting with this dreamlike unreality, the true reality of the world will become apparent in the days of *Mashiach.* As steps in this direction, our entire service of G-d, both through Torah study and through the observance of the *mitzvos,* should thus be directed to constructing G-d's dwelling on earth, which will attain completion in the days of *Mashiach.*[66]

---

64. See *Tanya,* ch. 23.
65. *Ibid.,* ch. 37.
66. Through the observance of *mitzvos* the dwelling place in the lower worlds is in fact being built now (in the time of *galus*), but it will become manifest only in the days of *Mashiach.* See *Likkutei Sichos,* Vol. V, p. 240.

"I HAVE
COME TO
MY GARDEN"

These constructive steps are the opening theme of the last discourse published by the Previous Lubavitcher Rebbe, R. Yosef Yitzchak Schneersohn (the Rebbe Rayatz), before his passing on *Yud* Shvat 5710 [1950].[67] This *maamar*, entitled *Basi LeGani*, opens with a quotation from the Song of Songs:[68] "I have come to My garden, My sister, My bride." And the comment of the *Midrash* on this verse provides the *maamar* with a starting point for its discussion of the ultimate purpose of Creation.

The *Midrash* enables one to appreciate that *Shir HaShirim* is not a simple love song; rather, it is a sustained metaphor describing the ongoing relationship between G-d and His people. The above verse, for example, which speaks of G-d's return to His garden, alludes to the time of the construction of the *Mishkan*, the Sanctuary in the wilderness, for then the *Shechinah*, the Divine Presence, was again revealed on earth. The *Midrash* points out further that the word גני *(gani* — "My garden"), especially in the possessive form, suggests the privacy of גנוני *(genuni* — "My bridal chamber"). From this perspective, the verse relays this message: "I have come into My bridal chamber, to the place in which My essence was originally revealed."

The *Midrash* continues: "In the beginning, the essence of the *Shechinah* was apparent in this lowly world. However, in the wake of the [cosmic] sin of the Tree of Knowledge, the *Shechinah* departed from the earth and rose into the heavens. Later, on account of the sin of Cain and then of Enosh, the *Shechinah* withdrew even further from this world, rising from

---

67.   See the annotated English translation entitled *Basi LeGani* (Kehot, N.Y., 1990), prepared for publication by Sichos In English.
68.   *Shir HaShirim* 5:1.

the nearest heaven to the second, and then to the third. Later yet, the sins of the generation of the Deluge caused it to recede from the third heaven to the fourth, and so on.... [After the sins of seven generations had caused the *Shechinah* to withdraw seven spiritual levels from its initial manifestation in this world], seven *tzaddikim* arose whose service of G-d drew the Divine Presence down once more into this world below. Through the merit of Avraham the *Shechinah* was brought down from the seventh heaven to the sixth, through the merit of Yitzchak the *Shechinah* was brought down from the sixth heaven to the fifth, and so on — until Moshe, the seventh of these *tzaddikim*,... drew the revelation of the *Shechinah* down once again into this world below."

Now, how can one speak of the Divine Presence withdrawing or retreating from this world? After all, the continuous Creator of the universe is of necessity constantly present in it: were He for one moment to withhold the input of His creative life-force from the universe, it would cease to exist.[69] "Presence" and "withdrawal" therefore really relate to whether or not the world *feels* G-d's nearness, for sometimes the spirit of folly which persuades a man to sin can camouflage the truth and dull his spiritual sensitivity. In this sense, then, the Divine Presence can be said to have withdrawn.

A *tzaddik*, through his Divine service, can bring that Presence back to the world. Thus, as recounted above, it was Moshe Rabbeinu, the seventh of the early *tzaddikim*, who finally brought the *Shechinah* to rest in the *Mishkan*.

The centrality of this event is reflected in the contents of the *Chumash*, the Five Books of Moses. Its narrative begins with creation and continues with the Egyptian bondage and redemption. Thereafter, surprisingly, it is predominantly occupied with the travails of the forty years of wandering in the

---

69. *Tanya — Shaar HaYichud VehaEmunah*, ch. 2; see *Lessons In Tanya* (Kehot, N.Y., 1989), Vol. III, p. 843ff.

desert, the building of the *Mishkan,* and the sacrifices.[70]
Moreover, it ends abruptly with the death of Moshe and leaves
the account of the people's entry to the Land for the Book of
Yehoshua (Joshua).

The lesson is simple. The Torah is pointing to the purpose
of creation. The early stages of its narrative are thus merely a
prelude to Sinai, where the Torah was given in order to enable
man below to build G-d a dwelling place, as embodied in the
physical *Mishkan.* This progression encapsulates a directive for
our entire history: In whatever spiritual wilderness a Jew may
find himself, his task is to build a *Mishkan,* a place where the
Divine Presence can feel at home.

FIRST,
SECOND —
AND THIRD

A further stage in this historical progression towards creating the perfect Divine dwelling place was the construction in
Jerusalem of the first *Beis HaMikdash* and then the Second.
Our people's sinfulness, however, brought about their destruction, leaving the task of construction unfinished — until the
long exile in which we still find ourselves will finally end when
Mashiach comes and builds the Third *Beis HaMikdash.* At that
point, the Divine Presence will again be revealed in the world.

Without this revelation, Judaism is incomplete. For one
thing, only in the Messianic Era will it be possible to properly

---

70.   In the above-quoted *maamar* entitled *Basi LeGani,* the Rebbe Rayatz
        explains how the Divine service of offering sacrifices in the *Mishkan*
        (and later in the *Beis HaMikdash*) parallels today's continuing Divine
        service of sacrificing the animal soul within man. This elevation of
        man's animalistic nature is essential to the process of constructing
        G-d's dwelling place, for this must be located even in the "lowest"
        elements of Creation, i.e., in our animal souls. (On the animal and
        Divine souls within man see *Tanya,* chs. 1 and 2.)

observe all the *mitzvos*.[71] Waiting and yearning for *Mashiach* is therefore a natural feeling for a Jew. Believing and waiting for him to come is a fundamental principle of the faith. For the coming of *Mashiach* is not only a reward but a fulfillment of the purpose of creation.

This manifestation of the Divine Presence in the physical world, which constitutes the consummation of Creation, is no novelty, for this lowly world was the dwelling place of the *Shechinah* from the beginning of Creation.[72] How can that manifestation now be renewed? The Rebbeim of *Chabad-Lubavitch* have taught that the urgent task of our era is to disseminate the teachings of Torah and *Chassidus* in every corner of the world.[73]

Contemplating this formidable challenge, a mere individual might well argue: Since this world has apparently been created so evil that it is[74] "full of *kelipos* and *sitra achara*," how possibly could (or should) he have any effect on it? Would it not be more productive and more inviting to confine oneself, uninterrupted and unchallenged, to tranquil halls of study...?

This argument, however, is unfounded. For the above *Midrash* indicates that the evil which is so prevalent in the world is not part of its essence, but rather a component that was added as a result of the sin of Adam. Indeed, this lowly physical world enjoys a paradoxical superiority over the "higher" worlds in that this was the main resting place of the *Shechinah*. And since the world is created anew *ex nihilo* every

---

71.   Cf. ch. 11 below. See *Likkutei Sichos,* Vol. XXI, p. 114; Vol. XXVI, p. 225; Vol. XXXIV, p. 114ff.
72.   *Likkutei Sichos,* Vol. VI, p. 81ff.
73.   On Rosh HaShanah, 5507 (1746), when the soul of the Baal Shem Tov — the founder of Chassidism — ascended to the heavenly abode of *Mashiach,* he asked: "Master, when will you come?" And *Mashiach* replied, "When the wellsprings of your teachings will be disseminated far and wide." (See *Keser Shem Tov* (Kehot, N.Y.), p. 3.)
74.   *Tanya,* ch. 36.

single second[69] because of G-d's desire to have a dwelling place in this world, no action of man can hold back the ultimate revelation which will fulfill G-d's purpose.

In time to come, when[75] "I shall remove the spirit of evil from the earth," every created being will *see* that the Divine Presence has returned to its original abode. Since the intermediate condition is reversible, it is not halachically considered a change.[76] In truth the world is thus now, even in its present state, a dwelling place for the *Shechinah,* and our task is to make that inner truth manifest. As we pray on Rosh HaShanah,[77] "May everything that has been made know that You have made it." Or, in the words of the prophetic promise, in time to come[78] "the world will be filled with the knowledge of G-d as the waters cover the ocean bed."

At that time, moreover, we will be able to perceive the function of evil from a more charitable perspective. In the past, the creation of evil has always appeared to constitute a steep descent in the world's spiritual history. Yet evil was created in order that its darkness should eventually be transformed to light, thus enabling the *Shechinah* to be sensed. In future time, therefore, the creation of evil will be perceived as having been a positive and necessary stage in the ascent that will come about through its transformation.[79]

The next chapter further explores this developmental process of revelation by first defining the meaning of "the World to Come."

---

75. *Zechariah* 13:2.

76. *Sukkah* 30b; *Bava Kama* 86b.

77. *Machzor for Rosh HaShanah with English Translation* (trans. R. Nissen Mangel; Kehot, N.Y., 1983), p. 32.

78. *Yeshayahu* 11:9.

79. See *Likkutei Sichos,* Vol. V, p. 66.

CHAPTER 3

THE WORLD TO COME: WHY A BODILY RESURRECTION?

> **"All Israel have a share in the World to Come."**[80]

THE BASIC CONCEPTION

The above assurance is perhaps the most commonly quoted of the many Talmudic references to *Olam HaBa*, the World to Come. Yet there are two schools of thought as to what the *Talmud* means by this term.

Before these two views are distinguished, however, it should be noted that the following basic conception of the soul and its descent to this world is shared by all the thinkers concerned:

---

80. *Sanhedrin* 11:1.

The soul, being[81] "a part of G-d," is immortal: it exists both before its descent into the body and after its departure.

The purpose of the descent is twofold:[82]

(a) By serving G-d while enclothed in the body below, the soul is enabled to upgrade the status that it will enjoy after leaving the body. Its descent was thus undertaken for the sake of a subsequent ascent.[83] (Conversely, if the soul fails in its mission, it later finds itself below the level which it left before descending into the body.)

(b) The refining of the body and the physical world.

How is this done?

King Solomon says *(Mishlei* 20:27*):* "The soul of man is a lamp of G-d." But why does the Creator of light need a lamp? — Because since the world is dark, the soul of man (a spark from the Divine luminary) is placed within the body and the physical world in order to illuminate it. By thus revealing the hidden Presence of G-d, the soul constructs a dwelling place for Him.

The two schools of thought as to what the *Talmud* means by the World to Come may be outlined as follows:

THE
VIEW OF
RAMBAM

Rambam[84] maintains that the World to Come *(Olam HaBa)* is the World of Souls *(Olam HaNeshamos),* which is often

81.   *Tanya,* ch. 2.
82.   *Ibid.,* ch. 37.
83.   In the original, *yeridah tzorech aliyah* (cf. *Tanya,* end of ch. 31).
84.   *Hilchos Teshuvah* 8:8. See also: *Midrash Tanchuma, Vayikra,* sec. 8; Rabbeinu Bachya, *Chovos HaLevavos* 4:4; R. Yehudah HaLevi, *Kuzari*

referred to as the Garden of Eden *(Gan Eden)*. It is from this pool of souls in the spiritual realms that every soul departs when it is about to descend into a body, and it is to this same state that the soul returns when it leaves the body at the conclusion of its mission.[85] Ultimately, when the time comes for the Resurrection, this will be (as conceived by *Rambam*) a transient stage, for after the Resurrection the body will again die, and the soul will return to the World to Come, i.e., to the World of Souls.

THE VIEW
OF THE OTHER
MAJOR AUTHORITIES

In contrast to the view of *Rambam*, most authorities[86] hold that the phrase "World to Come" in the *Talmud* refers to the era of the Resurrection of the Dead. (This state is called *Olam HaTechiyah;* literally, "the World of the Resurrection.")

It goes without saying that both Resurrection and the World of Souls are fundamental concepts in the thinking of all the authorities concerned.[87] The difference lies in the following question: What is the ultimate good which the Jewish people will merit? Is it the spiritual World of Souls, as *Rambam* maintains, or (as conceived by most authorities) will that good

---

1:109; R. Yosef Albo, *Ikkarim* 4:30, 33; R. Yeshayahu HaLevi Horowitz, *Shnei Luchos HaBris: Beis David* 1:16d.

85. See also: R. Jacob Immanuel Schochet, *Mystical Concepts in Chassidism* (Kehot, N.Y.); R. Adin Steinsaltz, *The Thirteen Petalled Rose.*

86. Rabbeinu Saadiah Gaon, *Emunos VeDeos* 6:4 (end of sec. 47 and sec. 49); *Raavad* on *Hilchos Teshuvah* of the *Rambam* 8:8; *Ramban, Shaar HaGmul; Kesef Mishneh* 8:2; *Shnei Luchos HaBris: Beis David; Chida, Avodas HaKodesh* 2:41; *Likkutei Torah* by the Alter Rebbe, *Parshas Tzav,* sec. 2 of the second of the *maamarim* entitled *Sheishes Yamim; Likkutei Torah,* sec. 1 of the *Biur* on the first of the *maamarim* entitled *Shuvah Yisrael.*

87. See *Ikkarim* 4:31; *Kesef Mishneh* 8:2.

become manifest within the context of material reality at the time of the Resurrection of the Dead?

In other words, *Rambam* holds that after the Resurrection of the Dead, people will still die and inherit their ultimate reward in the World of Souls.[88] The other authorities maintain that after death all souls abide in the World of Souls until the Resurrection, at which time they are finally enclothed in a body and in that state are granted their ultimate reward.

It should be noted that this difference of opinion between *Rambam* and the other authorities was meaningful only in their days, for since the *AriZal* — whose pronouncements in the esoteric areas of the Torah have been universally accepted — ruled according to the majority opinion, this is to be accepted as the final *halachah*.[89]

The majority opinion, however, requires clarification. Surely spiritual rewards would be loftier if they were awarded to a soul that is detached (as in the World of Souls) from the limitations of a physical body! How could it be that, according to most authorities, the soul's ultimate reward will be in this world?

To rephrase the question: Why a *bodily* Resurrection? If the purpose of resurrection is spiritual reward, why reward the soul in a body, and not alone?

One could argue, that since the body plays a role in earning the reward, Divine Providence demands that the body too be rewarded: hence Resurrection. A Talmudic parable[90] illustrates this.

---

88. *Rambam, Maamar Techiyas HaMeisim* ("Discourse on Resurrection"), ch. 4.
89. *Igros Kodesh* (Letters) of the Lubavitcher Rebbe, Vol. I, p. 142, footnote 1.
90. *Sanhedrin* 91b; see also *Ritva* on *Rosh HaShanah* 16b.

A blind man and a lame man both desired to raid a certain orchard — but how? The lame man therefore climbed up on the shoulders of the blind man, and directed him there. When the owner caught them separately on their way out, each protested that he could not have stolen alone. The resourceful owner thereupon sat the lame man on the shoulders of the blind man, and administered their punishment together....

However, this parable explains only a certain level of reward that is appropriate to the soul as it resides in the body; it does not explain why the ultimate reward must involve the body as well. In other words, the above explanation could also be consonant with the view of *Rambam,* that Resurrection will be followed by an ultimate reward in the World of Souls. It does not suffice to explain the position of *Ramban* (Nachmanides) and the other authorities that the ultimate reward will only involve the soul in a body.[91]

As mentioned above, the Kabbalists[92] concur with this majority opinion, so we shall look to chassidic philosophy for a solution.

A CHASSIDIC PERSPECTIVE

In general terms, Resurrection may be viewed from two angles: (a) as the perfection of mankind, and (b) as an era of reward for man's efforts in fulfilling the will of the Creator.

---

91. See *Igros Kodesh* (Letters) of the Lubavitcher Rebbe, Vol. II, p. 66 (footnote).
92. *Zohar* I, 114a, and III, 216a; *Tikkunei Zohar* 10b; *Tanya,* chs. 36, 37. For a full discussion see *Derech Mitzvosecha* by the *Tzemach Tzedek,* p. 14b. See also: *Shnei Luchos HaBris: Beis David* 1:31b; *Ramchal, Derech HaShem* 1:3:9; *Chida, Avodas HaKodesh* 2:42-43.

In truth these two points blend into one, since man and the entire universe are created in such a way that they climb the ladder of perfection step by step. As man through his own efforts nears perfection, he is helped from above to attain a level which transcends his own limitations. To paraphrase the words of the Sages,[93] A man sanctifies himself a little below, in this world, and he is granted further sanctity from above, in the World to Come.[94]

Obviously, a reward is something that is perceived by the recipient as good. Indeed, it may be measured by the recipient's appreciation of it. For example: A worker may receive his reward in the form of bread and clothes. A student who has served his master may be rewarded by tuition. As a further reward, the master may reveal to him his purpose in creation and the pathway through which he can access this purpose.

Given that the everlasting wealth of spiritual possessions is superior to physical possessions, it is obvious that wisdom is a greater reward than food, and that the greatest of all rewards is to be shown the pathway to eternity. Man's body and soul, however, are created and therefore finite; moreover, the pleasure they experience and the rewards they can appreciate are likewise finite.

Some levels of goodness are within our range of perception and some are beyond. Beyond all other levels, is the level attained when one fulfills the commandments of the Creator, for a *mitzvah* connects finite man to his infinite Creator. (As explained in ch. 2 above, the root of the word *mitzvah* implies "connection".) Since there can be no greater good than being connected to the infinite G-d, the very performance of a *mitz-*

---

93.   *Yoma* 39a.
94.   In Kabbalistic syntax, this dynamic comprises three stages: a Divine initiative ("an arousal from above") elicits a mortal response ("an arousal from below"), and this in turn elicits a further arousal from above.

vah is in itself the greatest reward attainable. In the words of the *Mishnah*,[95] "The reward of a *mitzvah* is the *mitzvah*" — i.e., the *mitzvah* itself.[96]

The greatest kindness G-d bestowed upon man is that in the Torah He clearly showed the way to self-perfection. Indeed, the very word Torah stems from the word *horaah* ("teaching"),[97] for the Torah, G-d's directive to man, encompasses the entire life of man from his very first moment on.

The perfection of any entity may be gauged against the purpose for which it was originally created. What is the purpose of creation in general and of man in particular?[98] — "The Holy One, blessed be He, desired to have an abode in the lower worlds."

As mentioned in ch. 2, the self-screening process by which the infinite light of the Divine is attenuated by downward stages until a finite, physical world is created, is termed the *Seder Hishtalshelus*. The successive links that comprise this chainlike scheme are called "worlds", each of which progressively conceals the Essence of the Divine. The purpose of creation is not the existence of the "higher" worlds (such as the World of Souls) but this world of ours, which, in terms of revelation, is the lowest of all.[99]

---

95. *Avos* 4:2.

96. See at length the letter of the Rebbe Rayatz in *HaTamim*, p. 25.

97. *Zohar* III, 53b; *Maharal, Gur Aryeh*, beg. of *Parshas Bereishis*, citing the *Radak*.

98. *Likkutei Amarim — Tanya*, ch. 36, paraphrasing *Midrash Tanchuma, Parshas Naso*, sec. 16.

99. The terms "higher" and "lower" must be understood as standards of comparison that indicate to what degree G-dliness is revealed in each individual world: the more revelation, the "higher" the world; the more obscurity, the "lower". From this standpoint our material world is the very lowest, for here G-dliness is the most heavily veiled. See *Lessons In Tanya* (Kehot, N.Y.), Vol. II, ch. 36.

It is specifically in this world of spiritual darkness that G-d wished "to have an abode." This abode is constructed by the observance of the commandments, for a *mitzvah* is one of the means by which mortal man can connect himself with his Creator. When performing a practical *mitzvah,* man connects the material entity concerned, and at the same time his own animal soul, to G-d. In the terminology of *Chassidus,* this is called the revelation of the *Ein-Sof* (infinite) light in this world.[100]

This involves the transformation of *yesh* (lit., "there exists"), i.e., material and corporeal existence, into *ayin* (lit., "nothingness"). This elective self-nullification in the face of G-d's will allows His infinite light to become manifest in this world. It is thus the foundation of the Torah and its *mitzvos,* as it is written,[101] "G-d commanded us to perform all these decrees in order that we stand in awe of [Him]."[102] In other words, the Torah and its commandments were given in this world to a soul garbed in a physical body so that the bodily and worldly *yesh*

---

100.   In fact, the revelation in this world is more intense than the revelation in the higher worlds. The revelation there is only a contracted, concealed *emanation* of Divinity, whilst the revelation in this world is of the Essence. To explain: It was only the Essence of G-d that could create a material world in which it is possible (G-d forbid) for a created mortal to deny the existence of a creator. It is only the Divine soul — "a part of G-d", a "Divine spark" — which when garbed in the body, can refine and elevate the body and the world in which it lives. The same power that created this world, is the only power that can reveal its essence. The fusion of body and soul thus represents two opposites, G-d and the physical world. Through the observance of *mitzvos,* the soul refines and illuminates the body and the world, and reveals a level of light from the Divine Essence that outshines the light in the "higher" worlds (for this is merely an emanation). The ultimate reward for the soul can therefore be given only in this world.

　　　See *Likkutei Torah, Parshas Behar,* p. 42; see also *Likkutei Sichos,* Vol. XXX, p. 138, note 55, and Vol. XVI, p. 478.

101.   *Devarim* 6:24.

102.   See at length in *Likkutei Torah, loc. cit.*

should be transformed into *ayin* and thereby become a self-effacing receptacle for the light of Divinity.

Since the revelation of this light in the world is the purpose for which the world was created, it is clear that the intensity of this revelation will depend on the extent to which man elevates the physical world.

HISTORY
AS A
LADDER

Now, just as man matures in his abilities, progressing from easy tasks to the more difficult, so too in his capacity to receive a reward, he first has the ability to perceive a dimmer revelation of spiritual light — for this, as mentioned above, is man's true reward — and thereafter his perceptive capacity grows. (There were times in history when there was a G-dly revelation above and beyond the capacity of that particular time, such as at the Exodus from Egypt and the Giving of the Torah.)

In fact the entire created universe is advancing up the ladder of perfection and gradually becoming more refined. In terms of world history, this elevation has three rungs:

1. The present era.

2. The Messianic era.

3. The Resurrection.

In the first era, the period before the advent of *Mashiach,* the world is preoccupied with a constant battle between the forces of good and evil. Since man has been granted free will he may perhaps decide to do evil, at which point he will fall in spiritual level. He is also granted the capacity to undertake *teshuvah,* to return and repent, and thereby rectify his sin and be elevated to an even higher level than his previous state.

During the second era, the Messianic era, the battle against evil will have been won, redemption will replace exile, and man will return to the level of perfection that characterized Adam before the sin of the Tree of Knowledge.[103] The *sitra achara* (lit., "the other side," a Kabbalistic euphemism for evil) will still exist in the world — in the "mixed multitude"[104] — and this will affect the level of perfection attainable by the Children of Israel. The persistence of evil in the world explains the opinion of those who hold that all those living in the Messianic era will die (even if momentarily) before Resurrection, in order to be cleansed of this impurity.[105]

The days of *Mashiach* represent the zenith of what man can achieve by utilizing his own capabilities. At that time the Torah and its commandments will be observed[106] universally: "this day — to observe them," will apply not only to our current era but the Messianic era as well.[107]

103.　*Bereishis Rabbah* 12:6. See at length in *Avodas HaKodesh,* Vol. II, ch. 38.

104.　In Heb., the *eirev rav.* See *Tanya — Iggeres HaKodesh,* Epistle 26.

105.　See ch. 8 below.

106.　See *Torah Or, Parshas Vayechi,* p. 46a; *Toras Shmuel, Shaar Revi'i,* ch. 17. See also *Rambam, Hilchos Teshuvah* 9:2, and *Hilchos Melachim* 12:4 and 12:5 — though *Rambam* (12:2) reiterates his stance that "there is no difference between this world and the Messianic era except for [Israel's liberation from] the subjugation of the nations" *(Berachos* 34b). Cf. *Shabbos* 151b.

107.　*Devarim* 7:11; see also *Tanya — Iggeres HaKodesh,* Epistle 26.

　　　In contrast, see the comment of *Ramban* on *Devarim* 30:6. On the phrase *(Koheles* 12:1), "Years of which you shall say, 'I have no pleasure in them,'" the *Gemara* states *(Shabbos* 151b), "This refers to the Messianic era, when there will be neither merit nor guilt." *Ramban* understands this to mean that in the Messianic era there will be no free choice; rather, man will observe *mitzvos* naturally and spontaneously — and these are the years in which G-d has no pleasure.

　　　This interpretation is difficult to understand in the light of the explanation given in *Tanya* that the Messianic era will represent the ultimate in the observance of *mitzvos.*

In the third period, the period of the Resurrection, evil will be utterly eradicated. The world will know neither sin nor death, for[108] "in time to come G-d Himself will take hold of the Evil Inclination [and hence the Angel of Death] and slaughter it." In this period man will be granted a gift from above — perfection not only commensurate with his abilities but beyond them. There will be no more observance of *mitzvos*.[109] The righteous will sit with crowns on their heads and delight in the radiance of the Divine Presence.[110]

This reward will be granted to the soul garbed in a body, for at that time the original purpose for which the universe was created will have been fulfilled — to create a dwelling place for G-d in the lower worlds.[111] The developmental process of revelation[112] outlined above, proceeding from exile to the Messianic era and climaxing in the Resurrection, thus explains the necessity for Resurrection.

Alternatively, *Rashi* understands the above-quoted *Gemara* to mean that there will be neither merit nor guilt — since all will be rich. See also the comment of R. Yaakov Emden.

To resolve the matter one may possibly suggest that when *Ramban* refers here to the Messianic era he means its continuation after the Resurrection. This possibility, however, requires further clarification.

108. *Sukkah* 52a.

109. See ch. 11 below.

110. *Berachos* 17a. See also: *Rambam, Hilchos Teshuvah* 5:2; *Tanya — Iggeres HaKodesh*, Epistle 17; *Likkutei Torah, Parshas Shlach*, p. 47c; the Responsa entitled *Heishiv Moshe*, sec. 1.

111. After the Resurrection, "lower worlds" refers to the revelation of the Essence of G-d in the material world: such a fusion of opposites can be contained only by G-d Himself.

112. The necessity for a developmental process is explained in numerous sources in the literature of *Chassidus*. See *Or HaTorah: Bereishis*, p. 700; *Nach*, p. 36; *Shir HaShirim*, p. 771; *Devarim*, p. 858.

MAN'S
PERCEPTION
OF DIVINITY

Until this point, we have focused on this developmental process from the perspective of the perfection of man and his purpose in creation. Now, borrowing the language of chassidic philosophy,[113] we shall endeavor to explain in further depth the differences between these three stages from the perspective of man's perception and sensation of Divinity.

Speaking of his own experience Iyov (Job) says,[114] "From my flesh I perceive G-d," and the *Gemara* states,[115] "Just as the Holy One, blessed be He, pervades the entire world, so too does the soul pervade the entire body."

The life-force with which the soul nourishes the body is of three kinds. In ascending order: (1) the life-force that is apportioned to each of the various organs (e.g., the faculty of intellect in the brain, vision in the eye, and so on); (2) the faculty of will, which is not divided, but pervades the individual comprehensively; (3) the essence of the soul, which transcends the soul-faculties of both the above levels, and which is totally spiritual.

Since the coarseness and corporeality of the body conceal the spiritual nature of the soul, a man cannot actually experience the *essence* of the spiritual; he can only feel its existence through the soul-faculties that express themselves in his body.

True to the above-quoted analogy ("Just as the Holy One, blessed be He, pervades the entire world, so too does the soul pervade the entire body"), the Divine life-force in the universe is likewise of three kinds. In ascending order: (1) the level of

---

113. See: *Sefer HaMaamarim 5652,* the *maamar* entitled *Ein Aroch Lecha; Sefer HaMaamarim 5675,* the *maamar* entitled *Vayeishev Yaakov.*
114. *Iyov* 19:26.
115. *Berachos* 10a.

memale kol almin (lit., the Divine light which "fills all worlds"), i.e., the Divine Presence that is garbed within the created world and whose radiance is apportioned according to the level of each world; (2) the level of *sovev kol almin* (lit., the Divine light which "encompasses all worlds"), i.e., that pervades all worlds yet remains undivided (corresponding to the faculty of will in the body); (3) the Essence of G-d that utterly transcends the worldly dimension. (The levels of *memale kol almin* and *sovev kol almin* subdivide many times over.)

As in the analogy of the body, we creatures of this material world cannot perceive the quality of the G-dly light, even at the level of *memale kol almin*. It is only through G-d's works (such as the heavenly bodies) that we know of His existence; in the words of the prophet,[116] "Raise your eyes heavenward and see Who created these." In the World of Souls — the Garden of Eden in which the physical body does not conceal or interfere — the soul actually experiences the level of *memale kol almin*. Beyond that, during the Messianic era, when the physicality of the created universe will be refined and the Image of G-d will radiate within man as it did before the sin of Adam, there will be a revelation at the level of *sovev kol almin*. The ultimate stage will come with the Resurrection, when the Essence of G-d will be revealed.[117]

The *Tzemach Tzedek*[118] explains further that the light of the Garden of Eden, however sublime, cannot be revealed in physicality, whereas the light of the Essence, being unlimited, can be revealed even in physicality — in the spirit of the Kab-

---

116.   *Yeshayahu* 40:26.

117.   See also *Likkutei Sichos*, Vol. XXIV, p. 56, footnote 85, where the Rebbe suggests that the Divine revelation at the time of the "dance of the *tzaddikim*" (*Taanis* 31a) will take place in the Garden of Eden that will be located in this world after the Resurrection. Cf. *Likkutei Sichos*, Vol. XXIV, p. 66, footnote 76.

118.   *Derech Mitzvosecha*, pp. 28-30; see also *Or HaTorah: Bereishis*, p. 183, 700; *Shmos — Beis*, p. 583; *Nach*, p. 36.

balistic principle that "that which is higher descends lower." This explains why at the time of the Resurrection even Moshe Rabbeinu and the Patriarchs will be obliged to descend from the Garden of Eden for the Resurrection (even though they have been proceeding there from strength to strength for thousands of years) — for the level of Divinity that they perceive in the Garden of Eden, however lofty, is still limited, whereas at the time of the Resurrection the light of the Essence will be revealed.[119]

SUMMARY

Resurrection thus involves both a perfection in the state of man and a revelation of the Essence of G-d, and both these ideal states fuse in fulfillment of the purpose of creation. Hence the necessity for bodily Resurrection.

A final point: The Alter Rebbe explains[120] that G-d chose the Jewish people not only on account of the exalted nature of the Jewish soul, but rather on account of the material body, which outwardly resembles the bodies of the other nations. By virtue of this choice the body retains an element of eternity, for despite its eventual decomposition, the *luz* bone (see ch. 9) lasts forever, and from it the body will ultimately be reconstructed.[121]

---

119.   *Or HaTorah: Bereishis,* p. 225b. On the difference between the Garden of Eden and the period of the Resurrection as discussed in the teachings of *Chassidus,* see: *Tanya — Iggeres HaKodesh,* Epistle 17; *Torah Or, Parshas Yisro,* p. 73b; *Likkutei Torah, Parshas Shlach,* p. 46d; *Derech Mitzvosecha,* p. 14b; *Or HaTorah — Siddur,* p. 350; *Sefer Ha-Maamarim 5672,* Vol. II, p. 779; *Sefer HaMaamarim — Kuntreisim,* Vol. II, p. 422; *Sefer HaMaamarim 5700,* p. 44.

120.   *Tanya,* ch. 49; see also *Toras Shalom,* p. 120.

121.   *Likkutei Sichos,* Vol. VI, p. 84. See at length Appendix 2 below.

Chapter 4

Reincarnation

> **"Every soul of Israel needs to be reincarnated[122] many times, in order to fulfill all 613 commandments of the Torah in thought, speech and action."[123]**

The Commandments

The above chapter outlined the view of almost all the major authorities that the soul, after ascending from the body to the World of Souls for judgment and reward, will again be brought down *into the body* at the time of the Resurrection. This chapter deals with the concept of reincarnation.

---

122. The Heb. noun is *gilgul.*
123. The *AriZal,* paraphrased in *Tanya — Iggeres HaKodesh,* Epistles 7, 29.

The *Zohar*[124] clearly states that a soul may descend to this world more that once. Moreover, the *AriZal* writes[123] that every Jew needs to be reincarnated repeatedly, until he has fulfilled all 613 commandments of the Torah at the level of thought, of speech and of action.[125]

SUCCESSIVE DESCENTS

Accordingly, one might ask, if a particular soul has been reincarnated in a number of bodies, in which body will it be clothed at the time of the Resurrection?[126]

The *AriZal*[127] explains that each time a soul descends to this world, one of its components is rectified; through successive descents, the soul as an entirety is rectified. Ultimately, each component of the soul will be resurrected in the body which served as its host.

---

124.   I, 131a; *Tikkunei Zohar* 40. See also: *Tikkunei Zohar* 70:132a; R. Chaim Vital, *Shaar HaMitzvos;* Introduction to *Shaar HaGilgulim,* sec. 11; *Sefer HaBahir,* sec. 58 (195).

125.   "Excepted are the commandments incumbent only upon a king, because he discharges the obligation of all Israel, as he is a corporate collective of them all." See *Iggeres HaKodesh,* Epistle 29, in *Lessons In Tanya,* Vol. V, and footnotes there.

126.   This question is asked by the *Zohar* itself (I, 131a), and two answers are presented. However, the *AriZal* quotes (and hence apparently accepts) only the view of R. Yosei, as quoted above. See *Ramaz* on the *Zohar.* See also: *Tzlach* on *Berachos* 58b, *Maggid Meisharim* on *Parshas Mikeitz,* p. 15a. The *Zohar* (II, 100a) suggests that the soul will be resurrected in the body in which most of its work was accomplished; hence, in the most refined body. See *HaMelech BiMesibo* (Kehot), Second Night of Sukkos, 5723 [1961].

127.   *Shaar HaGilgulim,* Introduction 4; *Likkutei Sichos,* Vol. XVI, p. 517. On the concept of rectification *(tikkun),* see *Tanya — Iggeres HaKodesh,* Epistle 7.

COMPONENTS
OF THE
SOUL

The concept of components does not mean that no one person will house an entire soul, for each component comprises within itself all the components of the entire soul,[128] since all souls emanate from one Source.[129] Thus, all souls were originally contained in the soul of Adam,[130] and later in the soul of Yaakov Avinu, after which there developed 600,000 souls which further divide into 600,000 sub-souls.

In answer to the original question, then: Even if a soul has been reincarnated a number of times, each host body will be resurrected.[131]

---

128. Supposing, for example, a man excels in observing the *mitzvah* of loving G-d and thereby rectifies the appropriate component of his soul.

Upon Resurrection, he will also have the ability to contemplate the greatness of G-d and thereby fulfill the *mitzvah* of "knowing" G-d; likewise, he will also be able to fear G-d. However, these soul-powers will be present only because he loves G-d and therefore wishes to fulfill His will in all other areas; or, in a deeper sense, because he loves G-d so much, he truly wishes to know His greatness and is fearful of doing anything that might separate him from Him Whom he loves. This concept is encapsulated in the Talmudic comment *(Sotah 31a)* that Avraham Avinu's fear of G-d, as described in the Torah, stemmed from his love of G-d. (See *Likkutei Torah, Parshas Masei,* p. 88d.)

129. See *Tanya,* chs. 2, 32, 37, and *Iggeres HaKodesh,* ch. 7.

It is often stated that the soul of R. Shimon bar Yochai was a spark of the soul of Moshe Rabbeinu, and Eliyahu HaNavi bore the same soul as did Pinchas, yet all agree that all of these persons will be resurrected.

130. The *Midrash* relates that G-d showed Adam all the *tzaddikim* of future generations who would stem from him, some from his head, some from his hair, and so on *(Shmos Rabbah 40:3).*

131. The subject of this chapter is resumed in ch. 5 below.

Chapter 5

Who Will Rise?

> **"N**othing can stand in the way of repentance."[132]

What of the Wicked?

The *Mishnah*[133] first states that all Israel have a share in the World to Come, but then proceeds to name categories of people who are excluded.

Do the wicked have a share in the World to Come?

After detailing which kinds of transgressors belong to the categories excluded,[134] *Rambam* concludes: "When does the statement that such an individual does not have a share in the World to Come apply? — When he dies without having repented. However, if he repents of his wickedness and dies a

---

132. *Rambam, Hilchos Teshuvah* 3:14.
133. *Sanhedrin* 11:1.
134. *Hilchos Teshuvah* 3:6-14. (See also *Margaliyos HaYam* on *Sanhedrin* 90a.)

penitent,[135] he will be one of those admitted to the World to Come, for nothing can stand in the way of *teshuvah*. Even if he denied G-d's existence all his days and repented at the last, he has a share in the World to Come. This is implied by the verse,[136] 'Peace, peace, to the distant and the near, declares G-d, and I shall heal him.' Any wicked person, sinner or apostate, who repents, whether overtly or in private, is accepted. This is implied by the verse,[137] 'Return, wayward children.' Even though he is still wayward, as is apparent from the fact that he repents in private and not overtly, his *teshuvah* is accepted."

WHAT OF THOSE WHO DO NOT REPENT?

If so, anyone who repents either privately or publicly before he dies will merit a place in the World to Come. But what of those who do not repent before they die?

The Talmudic, Midrashic and Rabbinic sources make it clear that they too will have a place in the World to Come.

1. In the first place, a righteous son may secure his wicked and undeserving father admission to the World to Come.[138] Conversely, we find[139] that King David's prayers granted his

---

135. In the original, *baal teshuvah*. This, incidentally, is the only correct usage of the Hebrew term. Strictly speaking, a person who today is loosely called a *baal teshuvah* should be called (as in *Shabbos* 68b) a *tinok shenishba bein haakum* (lit., "a child taken into captivity among the gentiles"): since his ignorance stems from circumstances beyond his control, he is obviously blameless.

136. *Yeshayahu* 57:19.

137. *Yirmeyahu* 3:22.

138. *Sanhedrin* 104a.

139. *Sotah* 10b.

rebellious son Avshalom access to the World to Come.[140] Moreover, the intercession of R. Yochanan[141] enabled even Acher[142] to be admitted the Garden of Eden, though he was neither a relative[143] nor a student.[144]

2. The *Talmud*[138] relates that even though Yehoyakim was a wicked king, he was atoned by the disgrace that his body underwent after death. Elsewhere, too, the Sages teach[145] that the indignity of a body after death is a sign of atonement, and this is stated without any mention of prayers offered by relatives or others.

---

140. From *Sanhedrin* 104a it is clear that a father cannot help his son in this way, whereas from *Sotah* 10b it appears that he can. To resolve this apparent contradiction, *Tosafos (Sotah* 10b) explains that a righteous son can help his father even without praying, whereas a father must pray for his wicked son. See also: *Reishis Chochmah*, the chapter entitled *Gidul Banim*, and *Chanoch LaNaar* by the Rebbe Rashab, p. 19.

141. *Chagigah* 15b.

142. I.e., R. Elisha ben Avuyah.

143. The Lubavitcher Rebbe (in *Igros Kodesh*, Vol. I, p. 143) explains why it was specifically R. Yochanan who prayed for Acher, though he had no family connection. The Sages teach (see *Chagigah* 15a, *Tosafos s.v. Shuvu,* citing the *Yerushalmi, Rus Rabbah* 3:13, *Koheles Rabbah* 7:8, and *Yalkut Shimoni* there) that the first of the many reasons for which Acher became a sinner was the fact that when his mother was pregnant with him, she was overpowered by the smell of meat of an idolatrous sacrifice, which she then ate. Might this not serve as an alibi for Acher? The *Talmud* states *(Yoma* 35b) that if anyone blames his poverty in this world for his ignorance, the Heavenly Court will cite the example of Hillel, who was extremely poor and yet spent his time in study. So too, the only person whose example could be used to point an accusing finger at Acher was R. Yochanan: his mother also ate such meat before he was born *(Yoma* 82b), yet he grew up righteous. It was therefore only R. Yochanan who could effectively pray on his behalf.

144. See also *Sifri* (end of *Parshas Shoftim*) regarding atonement for those who left Egypt by means of an *eglah arufah* (see end of *Sefer Chassidim*), but cf. *Igros Kodesh* (Letters) of the Rebbe, Vol. I, p. 144.

145. *Sanhedrin* 47a, and *Rashi* there.

Moreover, the *Jerusalem Talmud*[146] states that even Yera-
vam and his company, of whom the *Mishnah* says that they will
not be granted entry to the World to Come, were in fact admitted after their bodies had been consumed by fire many years
after their death.[147]

3. The following verse speaks of ultimate repentance:[148]
"For die we must, like water that flows on the ground and that
cannot be gathered up again; and G-d favors not a soul, but He
devises means that he that is banished be not cast away from
Him." Citing the closing phrase of this verse as an assurance
(that no one banished from G-d by his sins will remain banished), R. Shneur Zalman of Liadi writes[149] that every Jew will
eventually repent, either in this incarnation or another.

4. The Sages interpret Jeremiah's vision[150] of two baskets of
figs, one very good and one very bad, on the non-literal level of
derush, making use of the fact that the same Hebrew word
(duda'im) can mean either "baskets" or the fragrant plants
called mandrakes. To quote their words:[151] "The good figs
allude to the perfectly righteous and the bad ones allude to the
completely wicked, but lest you think that the latter may be
beyond all hope, observe the verse that states,[152] 'And the mandrakes *(duda'im)* give forth a fragrance.'" The case of the
wicked is never hopeless; at some future time, even the basket

---

146. *Kilayim* 9:3.
147. As to the citation in the *Talmud Bavli (Rosh HaShanah* 17a) of Yera-
      vam as an example of one who will be eternally damned, this could be
      regarded as describing his spiritual state when alive, without
      considering the atonement that he was later granted when his body
      was burned.
148. *II Shmuel* 14:14.
149. Both in the Alter Rebbe's *Shulchan Aruch (Hilchos Talmud Torah* 4:3)
      and in *Tanya,* end of ch. 39.
150. *Yirmeyahu,* ch. 24.
151. *Eruvin* 21a.
152. *Shir HaShirim* 7:14.

of seemingly worthless figs will, like the fragrant mandrake, give forth a sweet fragrance.[153]

5. The Sages[154] teach that even the sinners among Israel are as full of *mitzvos* as a pomegranate is full of seeds; they, too, will therefore have a share in the World to Come.[155]

6. The Kabbalistic classic entitled *Emek HaMelech* writes:[156] "Now children, listen to me, I will teach you the fear of G-d, and His holy love for us.... Why does G-d trouble Himself with the wicked who anger Him at every possible moment? There are two answers: (1) Even though they are utterly wicked, there are sparks of holiness in them...; their soul which is a part of G-d is eternal...; He breathed it into them; (2) the handiwork of G-d lasts forever and can never cease.[157] It is this second reason that was the point of the patriarch Abraham's prayer when G-d showed him Gehinom and Exile through

---

153.   See also: *Rashi* on *Shir HaShirim* 7:14; *Shabbos* 88b; *Tosafos, s.v. Chutz*, on *Bava Metzia* 58b.

154.   *Chagigah* 27a.

155.   In a parallel discussion *(Eruvin* 19a) the Sages comment on *Yeshayahu* 66:24, "And they shall go forth and look upon the carcasses of the men who have rebelled against Me": This alludes to the sinners of the nations, whereas the sinners of Israel will do penance in *Gehinnom*, from which Avraham Avinu will ultimately free them. The *Talmud* excludes one who had relations with a gentile woman, but *Tosafos (s.v. Chutz*, on *Bava Metzia* 58b) explains that even this sinner leaves *Gehinnom* after twelve months. However, *Tosafos (s.v Posh'ei*, on *Chagigah* 27a) excludes certain sinners, and see also *Tosafos* on *Rosh HaShanah* 17a.

156.   *Shaar Tikkunei Teshuvah*, end of ch. 3.

157.   In the original text, the author cites two phrases from *Yeshayahu* 60:21: "[The Jewish people are] the branch of My planting, the work of My hands...." The first of the above two answers is based on the former phrase, which likens the soul to a branch of G-d, and the second answer is based on the latter phrase, which affirms that the work of G-d's hands is eternal.

which all the wicked would be corrected, for He has mercy on all His creatures."[158]

This passage suggests that since the souls of the wicked are "part" of G-d, it is inconceivable that they will not eventually return to Him. It is through the troubles of the exile that this will be achieved. As *Rambam* points out,[159] based on the opinion of R. Yehoshua,[160] the Torah has promised that at the end of their exile Israel will repent.

7. Both *Midrash Shmuel*[161] and the *Alshech*[162] write explicitly that the A-mighty troubles Himself with correcting the wicked so that they too will eventually merit a share in the World to Come.

WHO HAS NO PLACE IN THE WORLD TO COME?

Some path, somewhere, is thus always left open for the footsteps of the wicked who seek atonement. At the end of time, moreover, all the wicked will in fact be granted a share in the World to Come.

What, then, is meant by the *mishnah* which declares that there are those who have no place in the World to Come?

A close scrutiny of its wording reveals its true intent:[163] "All Israel have a share in the World to Come, as it is said,[164] 'Your people are all righteous; they shall inherit the land for-

---

158. Similarly, see there in *Shaar Olam HaTohu*, ch. 31, and in *Shaar Ava*, at the end of ch. 46.
159. *Hilchos Teshuvah* 7:5.
160. *Sanhedrin* 97b.
161. Beginning of *Pirkei Avos*.
162. On *Parshas Shemini*.
163. *Sanhedrin* 11:1.
164. *Yeshayahu* 60:21.

ever; they are the branch of My planting, the work of My hands, in whom I take pride.' And these have no share in the World to Come:...'" — and those categories of people are enumerated in the passages that follow. Now surely one would have expected the *mishnah* to read, "All Israel have a share in the World to Come... *except...*"[165] The *mishnah*, however, does not use this word, which would present its two stances as outright opposites. How, then, can it enumerate categories of people who have no share in the World to Come if all Israel do have a share in it?

By way of a solution: The World to Come as mentioned in the *mishnah* refers (as discussed above) to the Resurrection, viz., the return of the soul into a resurrected body. When the *mishnah* says that all Israel have a share in the World to Come, it refers to the soul: all souls will eventually be resurrected, even the souls of the wicked, but not all bodies will necessarily be resurrected. As stated above, all souls are repeatedly reincarnated until they have fulfilled all the commandments. If a person was wicked in one incarnation, that body will not be resurrected; instead, his soul will be resurrected in a body that dates from one of its other incarnations.[166]

---

165. *Igros Kodesh* (Letters) of the Rebbe, Vol. I, p. 149, footnote 7.

 The entire thrust of the present chapter rests heavily on this comprehensive and closely-documented letter (beginning on p. 141), which the Rebbe wrote in 5703 [1943] in response to the query of a private individual.

166. As explained in the above-quoted source, the *mishnah* is to be understood as follows: "All Israel have a share in the World to Come..." — this refers to the souls; "and these have no share..." — this refers to those bodies that will not merit the Resurrection. Since the two parts of the *mishnah* thus speak of two diverse subjects, it is obvious that it would be inappropriate to say "except."

 Suppose it were to be argued that the *mishnah* says "and these" and not "except" because, after having interpolated a prooftext from *Yeshayahu*, it was obliged to resume its theme by reiterating a phrase that recalls its opening statement. The reply: Parallel cases in the opening *mishnah* of *Zevachim* and of *Menachos* (and see also *Yevamos*

The above explanation, which builds on the writings of the *AriZal*,[167] is based on the premise that the soul is cleansed

---

2:5) likewise interpolate explanatory matter between a general principle and its exceptions, but still revert to the exception with
"except".

Alternatively, it might be argued that the *mishnah* finds it appropriate to introduce its lengthy list (of those who do not have a share in
the World to Come) not simply and briefly with "except", but with a
more portentous phrase. The reply: In a parallel case at the very
beginning of Tractate *Chagigah* (and likewise in the above-mentioned
citations from *Zevachim* and *Menachos*), the word "except" is nevertheless used.

It is thus clear that the expression *"and these* [have no share in the
World to Come]" is used advisedly because — unlike "except" — it
does not connote utter exclusion. Since it expresses a more temperate
reservation, it allows us to understand that in each of the cases enumerated only the body will not return, whereas the soul will be resurrected, since all Israel have a share in the World to Come.

167.   *Shaar HaGilgulim*, Introduction 11, and *Sefer HaGilgulim*, ch. 5.

Other contradictions, too, may be resolved by this explanation. For
example: The *Talmud* (in *Sanhedrin* 107b) states that the generation
that built the Tower of Babel (and was thereafter dispersed throughout
the world) have no share in the World to Come. As pointed out by the
Rebbe Maharash (in *Toras Shmuel, Shaar* 6, ch. 14, and also in the
derush on *Parshas Tzav*, 5639), this would appear to contradict the
statement in *Pri Etz Chaim (Shaar Chag HaMatzos*, ch. 1) that the
Jews in Egypt were a reincarnation of that generation. Perceived from
the above perspective, the seeming contradiction disappears: The
bodies of that generation will indeed not be resurrected; their souls,
however, were refined and elevated in Egypt.

The same perspective can resolve another apparent anomaly: R.
Akiva *(Sanhedrin* 11:3) teaches that the generation that wandered in
the Wilderness will have no place in the World to Come, whereas the
writings of the *AriZal (Shaar HaLikkutim, Shmos* 3:4; *Shaar HaGil-*
gulim, Introduction 20) state that the generation of the Wilderness will
be reincarnated in the generation before *Mashiach* comes. (In *Sefer*
Asarah Maamaros, Maamar Chikur Din 2:8, the view of R. Akiva is
explained differently.)

The same distinction between the sometimes separate destinies of
soul and body is to be found in the commentary of *Mikdash Melech* on
the *Zohar* (III, 276a) that explains the statement of the above-quoted
mishnah in *Sanhedrin* (11:3) that the Spies have no share in the World

through the process of reincarnation even more than through
Gehinnom.[168]

KARES: THE
PUNISHMENT
OF EXCISION

The plain meaning of this punishment, which the Torah
reserves for a limited number of serious offenses (including
breaking the fast of Yom Kippur), is that the soul is cut off.
This is further implied by a statement of the Sages[169] regarding
excision both in this world[170] and the next.

Rambam defines it as follows:[171] "The reward of the righteous is that they will merit this bliss [i.e., the World to Come]
and take part in this good. The retribution of the wicked is that
they will not merit this life, but will be cut off and will die.
Whoever does not merit this life is truly dead and will not live
forever, but will be cut off in his wickedness and perish like a
beast. This is the *kares* of which the Torah writes,[172] 'That soul
shall surely be cut off.' [Considering the dual form of the verb,

---

to Come: though their bodies will not be resurrected, their souls will
be. (This resolution also solves the problem raised by *Nitzutzei Oros* on
the *Zohar* there.)

The teaching of the *Jerusalem Talmud (Kilayim 9:3)* on Yerovam,
that was mentioned early in this chapter, may also be interpreted in
this light.

See also *Igros Kodesh* (Letters) of the Rebbe, Vol. I, p. 149, footnote 8.

168. *Reishis Chochmah, Shaar HaYirah,* end of ch. 3, in the name of the
Ramak; see also *Shiur Komah,* ch. 84. See also ch. 4 above.
169. *Sanhedrin* 64b, reflected in the quotation from *Rambam* below.
170. In former times, a person punishable by *kares* would die before
reaching the age of fifty *(Moed Katan 28a, and see Tosafos there).* In
Tanya — Iggeres HaTeshuvah, ch. 5ff., the Alter Rebbe defines the
Kabbalistic sense of *kares* and explains why this is not evident today.
171. *Hilchos Teshuvah* 8:1.
172. *Bamidbar* 15:31.

hikares tikares,] the oral tradition explains: *hikares* means that
the soul will be cut off in this world; *tikares* means that it will
be cut off in the World to Come. [Such] a soul that is separated
from the body in this world does not merit the life of the World
to Come. Rather, even in the World to Come it is cut off....

"The[173] retribution beyond which there is no greater retribution is that the soul will be cut off and not merit this life; as
it is written,[172] 'That soul shall surely be cut off: his sin shall
remain upon him.' This is the obliteration of the soul which the
prophets referred to metaphorically as[174] 'the pit of destruction,'
or[175] 'obliteration'.... All the synonyms for annihilation and
destruction are used to refer to it, for it is the ultimate annihilation after which there is no renewal and the ultimate extinc-
tion that can never be undone."

There were many who misinterpreted these statements of
Rambam as implying that a sinning soul would not undergo
punishment in *Gehinnom,* which is a state of purgatory in the
World of Souls. In fact this was one of the reasons for the pro-
posed banning of this work.[176] In its defense, however, *Ramban*
(Nachmanides) cited proofs that *Rambam* also believed in the
existence of other punishments, though he saw excision as the
ultimate and final punishment.

At the same time, a concept that left *Ramban* unconvinced
was the ultimate obliteration of a wicked soul. As he writes, it
is inconceivable that a sublime soul which is in fact a "spark of
G-d" should ever become extinct.[177]

---

173.   *Hilchos Teshuvah* 8:5.

174.   *Tehillim* 55:24.

175.   *Ibid.* 88:12.

176.   See the commentary of *Rambam LaAm* on *Hilchos Teshuvah,* p. 248.

177.   For *Ramban* in *Shaar HaGemul* — quoted somewhat differently in the
       Mefaresh on the *Rambam* — excision means that the Divine soul natu-
       rally wishes to return to its true source. However, since the coarseness
       of its experience in the body prevents it from doing so, in that sense it

MODES OF
RETRIBUTION

The Kabbalists offer an explanation which is something of a compromise. It is well known that the soul comprises (in ascending order) five levels:[178] *Nefesh, Ruach, Neshamah, Chayah, Yechidah* — and only the level of *Nefesh* can be affected by excision.[179]

As an alternative solution: One of the sources for the concept of everlasting retribution for the worst of the wicked is the Talmudic statement[180] that certain non-believers, informers and others "will descend to *Gehinnom* and be prosecuted for endless generations...; *Gehinnom* will eventually come to an end but [their punishment] shall not." According to the simple and classical interpretation of this teaching, though *Gehinnom* is only a means of correction for the soul, and at some future time it will no longer be needed, these sinners will nevertheless continue to suffer.

The respective authors of *Asarah Maamaros*[181] and *Emek HaMelech*[182] interpret otherwise: *Gehinnom*, which is a negative force, will come to an end, and these souls will eventually be reaccepted and purified.

---

is cut off. What remains problematic is the *Ramban's* forecast of everlasting judgment for the absolutely wicked and the non-believers, based on the statement of the Sages *(Rosh HaShanah* 17a) that "they will descend to *Gehinnom* and be prosecuted for endless generations...; *Gehinnom* will eventually come to an end but [their punishment] shall not."

178. *Bereishis Rabbah* 14:9; *Devarim Rabbah* 2:9.
179. *Likkutei Torah* by the *AriZal, Parshas Bo; Sefer HaLikkutim, Parshas Lech Lecha; Sefer HaGilgulim,* ch. 6.
180. *Rosh HaShanah* 17a.
181. *Maamar Chikur Din* 5:1.
182. *Shaar Tikkunei HaTeshuvah,* sec. 3; see also *Shaar Kiryas Arba,* sec. 152.

Combining the above explanation with the Kabbalistic view, it could be said that those in the most extreme of the above categories will be subjected to a long period of excision and will undergo the cleansing of *Gehinnom,* but when the time comes and *Gehinnom* has completed its mission in the universe,[183] they too will have been rectified and rehabilitated.

It is also in this light that the commentaries explain the teaching of the Sages,[180] that those who sin bodily "descend to *Gehinnom* where they are prosecuted for twelve months, after which their body ceases to exist and their soul is burned, and the wind scatters them under the feet of the righteous." Here, too, a superficial glance might well give the impression that the souls of the wicked will be destroyed. However, the above commentaries[184] explain that these souls will undergo a change of form: just as something burned returns to ashes, so too will the souls of the wicked be reformed — except that their standing will be far inferior to that of the righteous.

---

183.   At first glance, the suggestion that *Gehinnom* will come to an end would appear to contradict the Talmudic teaching *(Pesachim* 54a), that "the light that G-d created on the second day of Creation *[Rashi:* 'i.e., the light of *Gehinnom']* will not be extinguished forever." However, it is pointed out in *Asarah Maamaros, Maamar Chikur Din* 5:5, and in *Emek HaMelech, Shaar Shaashuei HaMelech,* ch. 1, that when the *Talmud* uses the expression *olamis* ("forever"), it does not mean "for eternity," but for the entire duration of this world *(olam* — lit., "world"). When, however, we move into the era of the World to Come, i.e., when G-d will remove all evil and the tranquillity of *Shabbos* will reign, then *Gehinnom* will also cease to exist.

184.   See *Ramban, Shaar HaGemul; Asarah Maamaros, Maamar Chikur Din* 5:7; *Emek HaMelech, Shaar Ava,* ch. 46.

THE
RESURRECTION OF
RIGHTEOUS GENTILES

The *Midrash*[185] states clearly that the Resurrection applies to Israel, while the commentary entitled *Yfei Toar* explains that it includes righteous gentiles as well. The *Zohar*[186] implies that the idolatrous nations of the world will not be resurrected.[187]

OVERPOPULATION

R. Saadiah Gaon[188] makes a calculation[189] that when the time comes the world will be extensive enough to accommodate all those resurrected. R. Yaakov Emden[190] dismisses this calculation: just as the Resurrection will be miraculous, so, too, at that time the earth will miraculously cope with all its inhabi-

---

185. *Bereishis Rabbah* 13:6.
186. I, 181b.
187. See also Rabbeinu Bachye, *Parshas Noach* 6:12, 11:10. Abarbanel, however, in *Maayanei HaYeshuah*, p. 11a, writes that Resurrection will apply to all of mankind. He notes two purposes in this: (1) It would be unfair to all the generations who hoped for the coming of *Mashiach* if only those who had the good fortune to be alive at that time would be privileged to enjoy the benefits of the Redemption. Therefore all the dead will be resurrected — the righteous to enjoy the benefits they merited, and the enemies of Israel in order to witness their own ultimate downfall. (2) The nations then to be resurrected will realize the folly of their beliefs and will acknowledge G-d's sovereignty, in the spirit of the prophecy that appears (for example) in *Zephaniah* 3:9: "For I shall then make the nations pure of speech, so that they will all call upon the Name of G-d and serve Him with one purpose."

   Other authorities, however, hold that only the righteous will merit resurrection; see: R. Saadiah Gaon, *Emunos VeDeos*, ch. 7; *Rambam*, *Peirush HaMishnayos, Sanhedrin*, ch. 10; *Ramban*, *Shaar HaGemul*, sec. 11.
188. *Emunos VeDeos, Maamar* 7:8.
189. Explained by *Mabit* in *Beis Elokim, Shaar HaYesodos*, ch. 59.
190. In his commentary on the *Siddur*, in the *Maamados* for Friday.

tants. In this spirit the *Talmud* often speaks of situations (such as in the courtyard of the *Beis HaMikdash*[191]) in which G-d's transcendence of space so completely permeated the physical universe, that a limited area miraculously held many people. The *Midrash* teaches even more specifically:[192] "When G-d told Moshe Rabbeinu to convene the Jewish people at the entrance to the Tent of Meeting, Moshe complained, 'A-mighty G-d: How can I possibly stand 600,000 men and 600,000 youths at the entrance to the Tent which is a plot of land that is only big enough to yield two *seah* of grain?' And G-d replied: '...So, too, in time to come, will I do the same in Zion: All the world's population from Adam until the Resurrection will come and complain about the shortage of space, and I will broaden it for them.'"

As to feeding such a population, the *Midrash* writes:[193] "He who brings the people will provide for them."[194]

SUMMARY

After undergoing various forms of rectification, including even reincarnation followed by cleansing in *Gehinnom*,[195] *all* Jewish souls — including the souls of the wicked — will eventually be resurrected, though not all bodies. The principle that "all Israel have a portion in the World to Come" thus refers to the souls. The teachings of the Sages regarding those individuals who will not rise at the Resurrection refer to the

191.   *Avos* 5:5.
192.   *Tanchuma, Parshas Tzav*, sec. 12.
193.   *Koheles Rabbah* 5:10. See also at length in *Emunas HaTechiyah*, ch. 6.
194.   Ch. 10 below cites the view that there will be no eating — for nutritional purposes — after the Resurrection.
195.   *Emek HaMelech, Shaar Tikkunei Teshuvah*, ch. 1.

bodies of the wicked, whose souls will be resurrected in different bodies.[196]

As to the delicate question of *who are the wicked,* we can do no better than conclude our chapter with the same quotation[197] with which the Rebbe chose to conclude his classic responsum on this subject:[198] "Blessed be G-d — the G-d of Abraham, the epitome of kindness — Who has not removed His kindness from His people Israel. None shall be left forlorn, for His mercy has no end, and[199] 'all Israel have a share in the World to Come'; as it is written,[200] 'Your people are all righteous; they shall inherit the land forever; they are the branch of My planting, the work of My hands, in whom I take price.'"

---

196. *Midrash Talpios (Anaf Chelek LeOlam HaBa)* cites a different interpretation in the name of Rabbeinu Bachye and Recanati: The statement of the *mishnah,* "And these have no share in the World to Come," means that these individuals have no recognizable share of their own, but they do benefit from the "storehouses of charity" that are reserved for those who did not merit a share in the World to Come.

    In his *Igros Kodesh* (Letters), Vol. I, p. 150, the Rebbe explains the teaching of the *Gemara (Taanis 7a)* that "Resurrection is only for the righteous."

197. From *Emek HaMelech, Shaar Reisha DeZa,* end of ch. 48.

198. *Igros Kodesh* (Letters) of the Rebbe, Vol. I, p. 153.

199. *Sanhedrin* 11:1.

200. *Yeshayahu* 60:21.

CHAPTER 6

WHEN WILL THE RESURRECTION TAKE PLACE?

> **"G**-d builds Jerusalem, He gathers together the outcasts of Israel."[201]

THE SEQUENCE OF EVENTS

Describing the advent of *Mashiach*, *Rambam* writes:[202] "If a king will arise from the House of David who, like David his

---

201. *Tehillim* 147:2.
202. *Hilchos Melachim* 11:4. Considering the elaborate length of his *Discourse on the Resurrection*, it is interesting to note that *Rambam* does not even mention this subject in his *Mishneh Torah*. A number of commentaries explain this by observing that the function of this work is to codify applicable *Halachah;* it does not discuss future events outside this context. Hence it does discuss the coming of Eliyahu Ha-Navi and *Mashiach*, for these have applicable halachic ramifications, as is documented in the commentaries.

ancestor, delves deeply into the study of the Torah and observes its *mitzvos* as prescribed by the Written law and the Oral law; if he will compel all of Israel to walk in [the way of the Torah] and repair the breaches [in its observance]; and if he will fight the wars of G-d; — we may, with assurance, consider him *Mashiach*. If he succeeds in the above, builds the *[Beis Ha]Mikdash* on its site, and gathers in the dispersed remnant of Israel, he is definitely the *Mashiach*."

We see from this ruling that *Rambam* holds that the Ingathering of the Exiles will follow the building of the Third Temple. This view is based on the verse,[203] "G-d builds Jerusalem, He gathers together the outcasts of Israel," and is supported by numerous Talmudic and Midrashic sources.[204]

Continuing this theme, the *Zohar*[205] quotes the verse in *Tehillim* that follows the above verse,[206] "He heals the brokenhearted and binds up their wounds," and writes that the Resurrection will take place forty years[207] after the Ingathering of the Exiles.

The order of events will thus be as follows:

1. The arrival of *Mashiach*.

---

203.   *Tehillim* 147:2.
204.   *Berachos* 49a; *Midrash Tanchuma, Parshas Noach*, sec. 11 (and see the commentary of *Etz Yosef* there). For full documentation, see *Igros Kodesh* (Letters) of R. Sholom Ber Schneersohn of Lubavitch (the Rebbe Rashab), Vol. I, p. 309.
205.   I, 139a; see also p. 134a.
206.   *Tehillim* 147:3.
207.   The *Zohar* draws a mystical analogy between this interval of 40 years and the 40 years of Yitzchak's age at marriage and the 40 years' sojourn in the wilderness. According to *Sanhedrin* 99a likewise, the Messianic era will last for 40 years. Commenting on this passage, *Chiddushei HaRan* cites the view that the Resurrection will take place 40 years after the arrival of *Mashiach*, and also cites variant opinions of 70 and 400 years.

2. The rebuilding[208] of the *Beis HaMikdash.*

3. The Ingathering of the Exiles.

4. Forty years later,[209] the Resurrection.[210]

---

208. According to many sources, it appears that G-d Himself will build the Third *Beis HaMikdash* (rather than *Mashiach,* as in the passage from *Rambam* which opened this chapter). It has been suggested, therefore, that the actual edifice will be restored by G-d, but its gates will be restored by *Mashiach.* For a full discussion of this point, see *Chiddushim U'Biurim* of the Lubavitcher Rebbe on *Hilchos Beis Ha-Bechirah,* sec. 19; and in English, *Seek Out the Welfare of Jerusalem* (by R. Eliyahu Touger; Sichos In English, N.Y., 1994), p. 145ff.

209. Cf. *Tzror HaMor* on *Shir HaShirim* 8:12, citing *Ramban.*

210. *Rambam's* apparent conception of two distinct periods within the Messianic era — an initial period conducted according to the natural order followed by a supernatural state of being — is discussed in *Likkutei Sichos,* Vol. XIV, p. 417. (See also footnote 56 there regarding the view of *Ramban.*) This discussion appears in English in *I Await His Coming Every Day* (Kehot, N.Y., 1991), p. 51ff.

   The Rebbe often quotes the *Zohar* to the effect that the Resurrection will take place 40 years after the advent of *Mashiach.* (See *Igros Kodesh,* Vol. II, p. 75; *Sefer HaSichos 5752,* Vol. I, p. 274. However, there are also other references in the *sichos* (e.g., *Likkutei Sichos,* Vol. XXVII, p. 206; *Sefer HaSichos 5733, Shabbos Parshas Balak,* footnote 3) — that if Israel merits it, Resurrection will take place earlier. (See *Yeshuos Meshicho* by Abarbanel, *Iyun* 1, ch. 3; *Maayanei HaYeshuah,* *Tamar* 2, *Maayan* 1; *Netzach Yisrael* by the *Maharal,* ch. 45.) The fact that *Rambam* does not mention the Resurrection in *Mishneh Torah* (see footnote 202 above) also suggests that in his opinion the Resurrection will take place at some time after the Ingathering of the Exiles.

   However, there are opinions that the Resurrection will take place *before* the advent of *Mashiach.* (See the commentary of *Yfei Anaf* on *Midrash Eichah* 1:51; *Likkutei Sichos, Parshas Vayechi* 5751, footnote 6, quoted also in *Shaarei Geulah,* Vol. II, p. 57; *Taamei HaMinhagim,* p. 470; *Maasei Tuvia* (by R. Tuvia the Physician); *Olam HaElyon,* end of sec. 47.) The *Halachah,* however, does not follow this opinion, since where there is a difference of opinion in the *Talmud,* the *Zohar* decides the *Halachah* (see *Sefer HaMaamarim 5709,* p. 184; *Likkutei Sichos,* Vol. XXIII, p. 102) and in this case the *Zohar* is clear in that Resurrection will follow the advent of *Mashiach* by 40 years.

According to one view, the Resurrection will take place in the month of Nissan.[211]

EARLY
RESURRECTION

There is an opinion that certain righteous individuals will be resurrected at the outset with the arrival of *Mashiach*.[212] As a reward for their lifelong divine service, they will thus be privileged to participate in the universal rejoicing that will accompany his arrival, and to witness the rebuilding of the *Beis HaMikdash*.

Similarly, there is an opinion that Moshe Rabbeinu and Aharon and his sons will be resurrected before *Mashiach* comes, so that they will be able to instruct the people as they did at the time of the Exodus.[213]

---

211. *Tur, Orach Chaim,* sec. 490, quotes Rav Hai Gaon in the name of the Talmudic Sages; see the Alter Rebbe's *Shulchan Aruch, Orach Chaim* 490:16. According to Rav Hai Gaon, the Resurrection will take place *before* the rebuilding of the *Beis HaMikdash.* (See *Otzar HaMidrashim,* Vol. II, p. 388.)

212. See *Zohar* I, 140a; *Chiddushei Ritva* on *Rosh HaShanah* 16b; Responsa of *Radvaz,* Vol. III, sections 1069, 644; *Migdal David,* p. 83a; *Biurei HaZohar* of the *Tzemach Tzedek,* p. 134. See also *Sichos Kodesh 5710* (Kehot), p. 100, and *Likkutei Sichos,* Vol. II, p. 518.

   Even according to this opinion the Resurrection of the righteous will take place in the Land of Israel, and those buried in the Diaspora will be conveyed there by means of underground conduits (cf. ch. 7 below). See at length in *Emunas HaTechiyah,* ch. 5. In *Sichos Kodesh 5714, Yud Shvat,* the Rebbe speaks of how the *Ohel* partakes of the holiness of *Eretz Yisrael* since it will be connected with these conduits.

213. See *Aruch LaNer* on *Niddah* 61b; *Tosafos* on *Pesachim* 114b; *Yoma* 5b; *Ikkarim* 4:35. *Midrash Rabbah,* at the end of *Parshas Eikev,* states that Moshe Rabbeinu will come together with Eliyahu HaNavi (the Prophet Elijah). Elsewhere, in *Parshas Vaes'chanan* 2:10, the *Midrash* states that Moshe was buried in the desert together with his people so that upon Resurrection he will lead them all to the Land. Combining

A related question: Can *Mashiach* himself be resurrected from the dead or does he have to be a man now alive?

Rambam[214] describes the revelation of *Mashiach* as a gradual process in the course of which a righteous and learned leader of his generation will fight the wars of G-d, become a potential *Mashiach,* and then go on to build the *Beis HaMikdash* and gather in the exiles.

However, there are indications that *Mashiach* could possibly be a righteous individual who has already lived and died and will then be resurrected as *Mashiach.*[215] Discussing the personality of *Mashiach,* the Sages state:[216] "If he is one of the living, then an example would be Rabbeinu HaKadosh [i.e., R. Yehudah HaNasi]; if he is someone from among the dead, then he is someone like Daniel."[217] Abarbanel, in his authoritative classic entitled *Yeshuos Meshicho,*[218] clearly raises the possibility that *Mashiach* may be among those resurrected. He cites a passage from Tractate *Derech Eretz Zuta:* "Nine people entered the Garden of Eden alive ...*Mashiach.*" He explains

---

these two *Midrashim,* it would seem that Moshe together with his whole generation will be resurrected and will appear with Eliyahu upon the arrival of *Mashiach.* (This opinion is cited in the Responsa entitled *Lev Chaim,* Vol. I, p. 32.) In *Hilchos Melachim* 12:2, *Rambam* notes that there is no uniform view as to exactly when in the Messianic process Eliyahu will arrive.

214. *Hilchos Melachim* 11:4.

215. On this sequence as described by *Rambam,* see the handwritten gloss added by the Rebbe to the printed draft of a *sichah* delivered on *Shabbos Parshas Tazria-Metzora,* 6 Iyar, 5751 [1991], footnote 45. It is reproduced in *Kuntreis Tzaddik LaMelech,* Vol. VI, p. 210.

216. *Sanhedrin* 98b.

217. Note *Rashi's* two explanations of this passage, and the comment of Ben Yehoyada. See also *Midrash Eichah Rabbah* 1:51 — "If *Mashiach* is among the living his name is David; if he is among the dead his name is David" — and the comment of *Yfei Anaf* there. See also: *Shaarei Geulah,* Vol. II, p. 57, footnote 6; article entitled "Everlasting Life" by Rabbi N. Davidson, in *Beis Moshiach,* No. 49, p. 34.

218. P. 104.

that according to this view, a righteous individual deemed to be the *Mashiach* will live, then die on account of the sins of his generation, but will eventually be resurrected. In his encyclopedic work entitled *Sdei Chemed,*[219] R. Chizkiyah Medini states that if Israel is exceedingly meritorious, *Mashiach* will be resurrected from the dead in a miraculous manner.

---

219. *Pe'as HaSadeh, Maareches Alef,* footnote 70. See also *Or HaChaim, Parshas Balak,* on the verse *(Bamidbar* 24:17), "A star shall shoot forth from Yaakov": "If Israel are found worthy, *Mashiach* will be revealed from heaven." See also: *Zohar* I, 203b; *Arba Meios Shekel Kessef* (by R. Chaim Vital), p. 68; *Shaar HaGilgulim,* ch. 13; *Meorei Tzion,* ch. 97; *Biurei Zohar* by the Alter Rebbe, p. 106b; *Biurei Zohar* by the *Tzemach Tzedek* and *Yahel Or* of the *Tzemach Tzedek* on *Tehillim* 82; *Or HaChamah* on *Zohar* I, 7b, and I, 212a. Note the closing phrase ("and he will redeem us") of the first *maamar* of the Rebbe (entitled *Basi LeGani 5711 [1951]),* translated by Sichos In English in *Basi LeGani: Chassidic Discourses* (Kehot, N.Y., 1990), p. 103.

CHAPTER 7

WHERE WILL THE RESURRECTION TAKE PLACE?

"I shall bestow glory upon the land of life."[220]

**DIGEST
OF A
DEBATE**

Both those buried in the Land of Israel and those buried in the Diaspora will be resurrected in the Land of Israel. Why should this be necessarily so?

The *Gemara* records a classic exchange on this subject, conducted entirely on the non-literal level of Biblical interpretation known as *derush.*

It opens with the following declaration by R. Eleazar:[221] "The dead of the Diaspora will not be resurrected, for it is

---

220. *Yechezkel* 26:20.
221. *Kesubbos* 111a.

written,[222] ונתתי צבי בארץ חיים — 'I shall bestow glory *upon the land of life.*' [This implies that] the dead of the land which houses [G-d's] glory shall be resurrected; the dead of a land which does not house [G-d's] glory shall not be resurrected."

To this R. Abba bar Mamal objects: "It is also written,[223] יחיו מתיך, נבלתי יקומון — 'The dead men of your people shall live; my dead body shall arise.' Does not 'the dead men of your people' refer to the dead of the Land of Israel, and 'my dead body' refer to the dead of the Diaspora?"

After noting the reactions of these two Sages to other verses that their colleagues then cite in support of either stance, the *Gemara* asks: Is it not unthinkable to suggest (as does R. Eleazar) that the righteous buried in the Diaspora will not be resurrected?

R. Ilaa answers this by saying that they will be resurrected "through *gilgul*"; i.e., their bodies will be (lit.) rolled through the ground.[224]

The question is then asked, "But is this not painful for the righteous?"

To this Abbaye answers: "Subterranean channels *(mechilos)* will be made for them."[225]

---

222.   *Yechezkel* 26:20, and see the *Targum* and commentaries there.
223.   *Yeshayahu* 26:19, and see the *Targum* and commentaries there.
224.   The *Zohar* (I, 128b) asks: "Who will take the bodies to the Land of Israel? — R. Yitzchak said, '[The angel] Gavriel will take them.'"
225.   In the original Heb., *mechilos.*

       The Rebbe points out that since the ground in which a *tzaddik* is buried will eventually be connected to the Land of Israel by channels, according to halachic criteria (set out in *Sefer HaSichos 5714, Yud Shvat*) it may even now be considered part of the Land. An awareness of this enables one to better appreciate the value of praying at the resting place of a *tzaddik*. See also *Kuntres HaHishtatchus, Maamarei Admur HaEmtzaei Kuntreisim* (translated by Sichos In English, 5755).

This, however, raises a question: If the righteous dead of the Diaspora will be included in the Resurrection, why did Yaakov and Yosef wish to be buried in the Land of Israel?[226] The answer is given, that they were not sure that they would be found worthy of being brought there through the subterranean channels.[227]

---

226. *Bereishis* 47:29-30; 50:24-25.

227. This answer is problematic, for if this is the reason, then all the righteous men of all the generations should have expressly asked to be buried in the Land of Israel. Were they all so certain that they would be found worthy of being brought there by means of the channels?

The author of *Noda BiYehudah* (*Mahadura Tinyana, Yoreh Deah,* sec. 206) was once challenged with this question with regard to the *baalei haTosafos*. He replied that perhaps it was not within their power to request that they be transported to the Land of Israel after their passing. Since, however, they were perfectly righteous, they would no doubt be preserved and would be found worthy of being brought to the Land in the way described.

The same author then proceeds to quote an alternative solution offered by his son. According to the opinion of *Tosafos* in *Kesubbos* 110a, there is no obligation in the present era (when there is no *Beis HaMikdash* standing) to migrate and live in the Land of Israel, since it is not yet possible to fully maintain the holiness of the Land and observe all of its distinctive *mitzvos*. For this reason, he argues, the *baalei haTosafos* did not want to be buried there.

This answer is difficult to understand, for the merit of being buried in the Land of Israel is independent of one's ability to observe its *mitzvos* during one's lifetime, as we clearly see from the requests of Yaakov and Yosef.

(By way of resolution: Perhaps this answer means that the *baalei haTosafos* did not choose to emigrate to the Land of Israel *in their lifetimes* because in our era one cannot fully observe its *mitzvos*.)

On the value of burial in the Land of Israel, see also the teaching of R. Anan in *Kesubbos* 111a: "If anyone is buried in the *Eretz Yisrael*, it is as if he were buried under the very altar." One of the prooftexts quoted is the verse *(Devarim 32:43)*, וכפר אדמתו עמו. Paraphrased in the spirit of the above-quoted *Gemara*, this means, "His Land will atone for His people." The same verse is cited by R. Eliezer in *Bereishis Rabbah*, sec. 96, in defense of an individual who lived his life in the Diaspora, but sought to be buried in the Holy Land: "Once he is

ANALYSIS

Which of these two positions does the *Halachah* define as authoritative?

The author of *Nodah BiYehudah*[228] rules (though without citing proof) according to the view of R. Abba, that those buried in the Diaspora will also merit Resurrection. However, since the discussion of the *Talmud* is based on the statement of R. Eleazar, and is supported by many of his colleagues, then according to the principles by which the *Halachah* is derived from the *Talmud*,[229] the *Halachah* is established according to his view. And indeed, this ruling is backed by sources in the

---

buried in *Eretz Yisrael*, G-d will grant him atonement." And since actual burial in the soil of the Holy Land is not always feasible, members of burial brotherhoods in the Diaspora are accustomed to place a little soil from the Holy Land in the coffin of the departed. On the sources and significance of this practice, and in particular its connection with the aspiration of the departed to be ultimately resurrected, see *Gesher HaChaim* by R. Yechiel Michl Tukatchinski, Vol. I, p. 299-301.

228. *Op. cit.,* sections 205 and 206.
229. Some authorities hold that these principles apply only to matters arising in the days of the *Talmud*. (See *Maharik, Shoresh* 185, cited in *Tosafos Yom-Tov* on *Kelim* 3:2; *Melo HaRo'im*, Vol. II, 300:21.) However, even those authorities concede that (a) these principles should be applied wherever possible, and that (b) the above restriction is relevant only when it is known that one of two disputants was more expert than the other in the field under discussion and for that reason the *Halachah* was fixed according to his opinion. (See, for example: *Bava Basra* 65a, with regard to R. Nachman's judicial experience; *Tosafos* on *Eruvin* 32a: the *Halachah* follows R. Sheshes in ritual prohibitions (Aram.: *issurei*) and R. Nachman in financial matters (Aram.: *dinei*); *Yad Malachi,* sec. 162: the *Halachah* follows Rav in *issurei* and Shmuel in *dinei* because, as the *Rosh* explains in *Bava Kama* 4:4, each was considered an expert in his field.) However, when discussing a principle such as a majority ruling (as in the case arising in our text), all agree that the above principles apply.

Jerusalem Talmud,[230] the *Midrash,*[231] and numerous statements in the *Zohar.*[232]

According to this opinion, the body will be reconstructed in the Diaspora, and only after making its way to the Land of Israel through the underground tunnels will it be invested with a soul.[233]

Moreover, since the *Gemara* says that the righteous buried in the Diaspora will be found worthy of *gilgul,* this implies that even according to R. Eleazar, the verse, "I shall bestow glory..." does not exclude the Resurrection of the dead of the

---

230.　*Kilayim* 9:3; *Kesubbos* 12:3.

231.　After citing one view that those buried in the Land of Israel will be the first to be resurrected, and another view that they alone will be resurrected, the *Midrash* (in *Bereishis Rabbah,* sec. 96) quotes the objection of R. Simmon: "If so, could it be that the righteous who are buried in the Diaspora should be deprived?! What, then, will G-d do? He will make subterranean caverns and they will roll to the Land of Israel, where G-d will infuse in them a spirit of life and they will arise. And how do we know this [i.e., that the Resurrection will take place in the Land of Israel]?"

　　In answer to his own question, R. Simmon cites the Vision of the Valley of Dry Bones *(Yechezkel* 37:12-14): "Therefore prophesy and say to them: Thus says the L-rd G-d: 'Behold! I shall open your graves and raise you up from your graves, O My people, and *I shall bring you to the Land of Israel.*'" Only then, observes R. Simmon, does the passage go on to say: "I shall put My spirit into you and you shall live...."

　　Resh Lakish adds: "It is explicitly written that as soon as the bodies reach the Land of Israel, G-d will infuse a soul in them, as it is written *(Yeshayahu* 42:5), 'He gives a soul to the people upon it [i.e., upon the Land]....'"

232.　I, 34b; II, 3b. However, the *Ramaz* comments on the former source that first the body will be resurrected in its place with the same soul it had in this world. Then, after undergoing the journey to the Land of Israel, it will receive a new soul. The difficulty in this explanation is that the *Ramaz* is commenting on a statement of R. Yitzchak, whereas on p. 128b, the *Zohar* quotes R. Yitzchak as saying that it is the angel Gavriel who will escort the body to the Land of Israel, and only after arriving there will it receive a soul.

233.　*Zohar* II, 3b.

Diaspora. It only tells us that the Resurrection will take place
in the Land of Israel, so that *all* those who are brought there
may also be termed the "dead of the Land of Israel" (with the
difference that the righteous will be brought there painlessly by
gilgul). When understood in this way, the view of R. Eleazar is
in harmony with the universally-accepted statement of the
Sages in *Sanhedrin,* that "all Israel have a share in the World
to Come."[234]

THE RESURRECTION: WHY IN THE LAND OF ISRAEL?

The *Zohar*[235] relates that R. Yehudah the son of R. Elazar
asked this question of R. Chizkiyah: "The dead that the Holy
One, Blessed be He, will resurrect, — Why will He not return
to them their souls in the place in which they were buried and
then bring them to live in the Land of Israel?"

R. Chizkiyah answered: "The A-mighty has sworn to build
Jerusalem and never to destroy it, for R. Yirmeyah has said:
'The Holy One, Blessed be He, will reconstruct His world and
build Jerusalem and lower it ready built from above[236] so that it
shall never be destroyed; moreover, He has sworn that He will
never again send Israel into exile, and He has sworn never to

---

234.   *Sanhedrin* 11:1; see also *Shaarei Geulah (Heichal Menachem),* p. 296.
       This concept is supported by the *Shelah (Shaar HaOsiyos,* end of the
       letter *kuf),* who paraphrases the *Gemara (Kesubbos* 111a) in these
       words: "R. Eleazar said, 'The dead of the Diaspora [i.e., not only the
       righteous] will be resurrected through *gilgul.*'" The same concept also
       answers the question of *Tosafos* in *Sotah* 5a.
235.   I, 114a.
236.   See *Rashi* on *Sukkah* 41a; *Tosafos* on *Shabbos* 15b; *Midrash Tan-
       chuma, Parshas Noach,* sec. 11; *Zohar* I, 183b, and II, 221a.

destroy Jerusalem.'[237] ...The dead will thus receive their souls in a place that will exist forever so that the soul will exist in a body forever."

The *Midrash* teaches, moreover, that in time to come Jerusalem will diffuse its sanctity over the whole of the Land of Israel, and the Land of Israel will diffuse its sanctity over the whole world.[238]

---

237. *Yeshayahu,* ch. 62.
238. *Yalkut Shimoni* on *Yeshayahu,* sec. 503.

Chapter 8

Who Will Rise First?

"Your dead shall come alive."[239]

GEOGRAPHICALLY

The Resurrection will take place in stages. According to tradition,[240] those buried in Israel will be resurrected before those buried outside Israel.[241] They will be followed by the generation who died in the wilderness.[242] Last of all will be the

---

239. *Yeshayahu* 26:19.
240. See *Jerusalem Talmud, Kilayim* 9:3 and *Kesubbos* 12:3; *Zohar* I, 113a; *Bereishis Rabbah* 96:7.
241. See ch. 7 above.
242. This is the view of R. Yochanan. However, one view in the *Zohar* (II, 168b) holds that the generation of the wilderness will rise first, and cites the verse *(Yeshayahu* 26:19), "Your dead shall come alive." Both the Babylonian and Jerusalem Talmuds understand this verse as giving precedence to those buried in the Land of Israel.

   At any rate, both opinions expressed in the *Zohar* hold that the generation of the wilderness has a share in the World to Come; i.e., they will be resurrected. This is in keeping with the opinion of R.

Patriarchs:[243] when they finally rise, their joy at encountering all their righteous descendants will be boundless.[244] The intervals between the various stages remain uncertain.[245]

PRECEDENCE

The righteous will rise before others,[246] and masters of Torah learning will rise before those who excel in the observance of *mitzvos*.[247] According to one tradition, the dead will be summoned by name in alphabetical order, except that precedence will be given to those who lived their lives in humility.[248]

What of those who will be alive at the time of the Resurrection? Will they live through it, or will they too momentarily

---

Eliezer, as against the view of R. Akiva (see *Sanhedrin* 110b, and *Tosafos* on *Bava Basra* 73b). The Rebbe explains this debate in *Likkutei Sichos,* Vol. XVIII, p. 248.

Regarding the time of the Resurrection of Moshe Rabbeinu and his generation, see ch. 6 above and footnote 12 there.

243.   *Avkas Rochel* 2:4 cites the view of R. Shimon ben Menassiah that the Patriarchs will be the first to be resurrected.

244.   *Ibid.*

245.   *Ibid.; Zohar* I, 139b; *Ibn Ezra* on *Daniel* 12:2; Responsa of *Radvaz,* Vol. III, p. 644, in the name of *Ritva,* quoted in *Ikrei HaDat* at the end of *Yoreh Deah. Chesed LeAvraham* 3:23 writes of a period of 40 years between the Resurrection of the dead in Israel and the dead of the Diaspora.

246.   *Zohar* I, 140a.

247.   *Ibid.,* p. 182a. See also *Biurei HaZohar* by the *Tzemach Tzedek,* p. 134.

248.   *Midrash* quoted in *Ohev Yisrael — Likkutim,* on *Parshas Berachah.* The *Mabit* (in *Beis Elokim, Shaar HaYesodos,* end of sec. 55) points out that according to this view Adam and Abraham will rise first since their names each begin with an *alef.* Alternatively, he suggests that perhaps the alphabetical order will apply only within each generation, while the Resurrection of each generation will take place in historical order.

die and be immediately resurrected?[249] In support of the latter view, it has been argued that since at that time G-d will remove the worldly impurity that precipitates death, the bodies of those who are then alive will be reconstructed to live forever — and this necessitates a momentary death.[250]

In brief, the answer to this question, too, will have to await the event.

---

249. See: Rav Saadiah Gaon, *Emunos VeDeios,* end of sec. 47; *Maavar Yabok* 3:3; the Rebbe Rashab of Lubavitch (R. Sholom Dovber Schneersohn), *Toras Shalom* (Kehot), p. 211. See also *Or HaChamah* on *Zohar* I, 116a, quoting R. Chaim Vital. See also Ben Yehoyada on *Sanhedrin* 92a regarding *tzaddikim* who were already resurrected upon the arrival of *Mashiach:* Will they have to die and be resurrected a second time? See also, in *Sefer HaSichos 5718,* the third *sichah* on Purim. See also footnotes to ch. 9 below.

250. *Zohar* II, 108b. See also *Likkutei Sichos,* Vol. XVIII, p. 409, footnote 71. Elsewhere (in *Sefer HaSichos 5718,* in the third *sichah* on Purim) the Rebbe explains that the momentary withdrawal will enable those resurrected, after their great thirst for the revelations of the Resurrection, to appreciate the "great light from out of the darkness."

CHAPTER 9

In What Manner Will the Resurrection Take Place?

> **"H**adrian once asked R. Yehoshua ben Chananya: 'From what will G-d resurrect man in the future world?'"[251]

THE DEW OF RESURRECTION

The bodies of the perfectly righteous do not decompose in the grave;[252] in the majority of cases only the skeleton

---

251. *Koheles Rabbah* 12:5.
252. See *Rashi* on *Devarim* 34:7, which speaks of Moshe Rabbeinu. On the phrase, "His eye had not dimmed," *Rashi* writes, "even after death"; on the phrase "and his vigor had not diminished," *Rashi* writes that "his life fluids remained within him: decomposition did not affect him."

remains.[253] There is a tradition that one small bone is inde-
structible. *Luz* is its name, and from it the body will be built at
the Resurrection.[254]

See also: *Shabbos* 152b, concerning R. Achai bar Yoshia; *Bava Basra* 58a, concerning R. Tuvi bar Masnah; *Bava Metzia* 84b, concerning R. Eleazar; *Kesubbos* 103a, concerning R. Yehudah HaNasi. See also *Midrash Tehillim* 119:9.

(Eye-witnesses to a similar case were still alive only a few years ago. Exactly twenty years after the Rebbe Rashab, the fifth Lubavitcher Rebbe, had been laid to rest in Rostov-on-Don in 1920, ten of his faithful chassidim risked their lives in order to exhume his body just before the old cemetery was bulldozed to make way for a Soviet housing project. They found his holy body intact, with only his *tallis* protecting it from the soil in which it lay, and reinterred it in its present resting place in the new cemetery in Rostov. Their contemporary account of this episode has been preserved by R. Moshe DovBer Rivkin, the late *Rosh Yeshivah* of *Torah VaDaas,* in *Kuntreis Ashkavta DeRebbe* (N.Y., 1953), pp. 145-8. In 1961, the editor of the present volume heard a first-person description of the episode from the mouth of one of the ten participants — the late Reb. Yonah Eidelkop, one of the venerable founding fathers of Kfar Chabad in *Eretz Yisrael.*

At the same time, the *Gemara* (in *Shabbos* 152b) and the *Zohar* (II, 108b) both hold that *tzaddikim,* too, will return to dust for a short while before the Resurrection, even though they may have lain intact for many years. The reason: Since the sin of the Tree of Knowledge tainted the world with evil, even the bodies of *tzaddikim* need to be refined. However, in a talk delivered on *Shabbos Parshas Bo,* 5748 [1988], the Rebbe explained that this stage does not necessarily entail a literal return to dust. It can also be understood as a spiritual nullification, in the spirit of the plea for humility that is made at the conclusion of *Shemoneh Esreh* (see *Siddur Tehillat HaShem,* p. 61): "May my soul be as dust to all." (See *Sefer HaMaamarim — Melukat,* Vol. II, p. 280.)

253. See the Responsa of the *Chasam Sofer* on *Yoreh Deah,* sec. 337, on this subject and on the *luz* bone. See also *Or HaTorah* (by the *Tzemach Tzedek*) on *Devarim,* sec. 858. On the underlying reasons for decomposition, see *Likkutei Sichos,* Vol. XVIII, p. 409, footnote 71.

254. *Bereishis Rabbah* 28:3; *Zohar* I, 69a and 137a; II, 28b; *Tosafos* on *Bava Kama* 16b. See also Booklet 7 of the recently-discovered *Reshimos* of the Rebbe, p. 14.

In the words of the *Midrash*,[255] "Hadrian once asked R. Yehoshua ben Chananya: 'From what will G-d resurrect man in the future world?'

R. Yehoshua replied, 'From the *luz* in the spine.'" Once G-d has softened this bone with the Dew of Resurrection,[256] it will become as yeast is to the dough, and from it the body will be built.[257] The same body that decomposed will be recon-

---

As recorded in the *Midrash* (in *Bereishis Rabbah* 14:5), Beis Shammai holds that the body will begin to take shape with sinews and bones, and the skin and flesh will follow; Beis Hillel holds that the Resurrection will parallel the formation of an embryo in this world, whose skin and flesh precede its sinews and bones.

255. *Koheles Rabbah* 12:5.

256. *Jerusalem Talmud, Berachos* 5:2 and *Taanis* 1:1. See also: *Likkutei Torah, Parshas Haazinu,* p. 73c; *Likkutei Sichos,* Vol. XI, p. 193, and Vol. XVIII, p. 252.

   The author of *Ben Yehoyada* on *Sanhedrin* 92a makes an original observation. Daniel is told by the angel *(Daniel* 12:13), "and you shall arise to your destiny at the end of days." In the original, this last phase is *ketz hayamin* — but *yamin* also means "the righthand side." In Kabbalistic terms, moreover, being "to the right" of something signifies not location, but progression. Now the letters that stand "to the right" of each of the four letters of the Divine Name *Havayah* are the letters which immediately follow them in the alphabet, namely כוז"ו. Significantly, their numerical equivalent totals ט"ל (*tal* — "dew"), and it is with this Divine Name that the graves will be opened.

257. *Zohar* I, 28b, and see also II, 169a. By contrast, *Pirkei deRabbi Eliezer,* ch. 34 (cf. *Zohar* I, 113a) states that the body will be reconstituted from decomposed matter in the grave. However, *Avkas Rochel* 2:4 and *Avodas HaKodesh* 2:40 understand this text as referring to the *luz.*

   To understand this discussion from the perspective of *Chassidus,* see: *Zohar* II, 83a; *Likkutei Torah, Parshas Masei,* p. 96b; *Sefer Ha-Maamarim — Melukat,* Vol. II, p. 460.

structed. This is implied by the verse,[258] יחיו מתיך — "Your dead people *shall live*" (and not "shall be created").[259]

As to identifying the *luz*,[260] some say that it is the coccyx,[261] a small bone at the base of the spine; others say that it is the bone at the back of the skull upon which the knot of the *tefillin shel rosh* is placed.[262]

CLOTHED, HEALED, REFINED

Some sources hold that the dead will be resurrected wearing the shrouds in which they were buried; according to others,

---

258. *Yeshayahu* 26:19.

259. *Bereishis Rabbah* 95:1; *Zohar* I, 115a, 126a, 130b, 203b; III, 91a, 216b. See also *Likkutei Sichos*, Vol. VI, p. 83, but cf. Vol. VIII, p. 248, regarding the two possibilities. According to the view that the reconstruction is based on the *luz*, the original body is reconstructed, whereas according to the above-quoted view of *Pirkei deRabbi Eliezer*, an entirely new body is resurrected. This also explains the statement in the latter source that the dead will be resurrected without blemish (in contrast to the statement in *Sanhedrin* 91b). See at length in *Emunas HaTechiyah*, ch. 2.

260. The *Midrash (Bereishis Rabbah* 28:3*)* locates it in the spine. See *Tosafos* on *Bava Kama* 16a-b, and *Bereishis Rabbah* 56:2.

261. See *Rashi* on *Bereishis Rabbah* 28:3; *Aruch, s.v. luz; Avodas HaKodesh* 2:40; *Avkas Rochel* as cited above.

262. *Likkutei Nach — AriZal, Parshas Shoftim;* see also *Likkutei Shas* on *Rosh HaShanah; Sefer HaMaamarim 5711*, p. 209.

      The above-quoted *Midrash (Bereishis Rabbah* 28:3*)* states explicitly that the *luz* is indestructible. (See commentaries of *Rashi, Matnos Kehunah* and *Yefei Toar* there.) Commenting on the verse (in *Bereishis* 2:22), "And G-d built the *tzela*," the author of *Tzror HaMor* writes in the name of *Sisrei Torah* that the bone is in the neck and is very hard; it will neither burn nor perish. And just as G-d built the body of Eve from a bone, so too will He reconstitute the body from the *luz*.

they will be resurrected in the clothes which they normally wore in their lifetimes.[263]

Though physical disabilities will carry over to the time of the Resurrection, they will be healed as soon as the bodies are reconstituted.[264]

Bodies when resurrected will be as refined as the body of Adam when he was first created — and even more so.[265]

263. *Niddah* 61b; *Jerusalem Talmud, Kesubbos* 12:3 (and the comment of *Yefei Mareh* there); *Tosafos* (and *Gilyon HaShas* of R. Akiva Eger and the comment of *Rashash*) on *Kesubbos* 111b; *Maharsha* on *Shabbos* 114b; *Radvaz* on *Rambam, Hilchos Avel* 14:24; *Radal* on *Pirkei deRabbi Eliezer* 33:77; *Sefer Emunas HaTechiyah*, ch. 4.

264. *Sanhedrin* 91b; *Bereishis Rabbah*, sec. 95; *Zohar* I, 199b, and II, 91a. Thus, too, the *Zohar* (I, 203b) — and so too the *Gemara* (in *Nedarim* 8b) — writes that in time to come G-d will take the sun out of its sheath and heal the righteous. (Cf. footnote 259 for contrasting views.) *Margaliyos HaYam* on *Sanhedrin* 91b lists further sources. See also ch. 1 above, footnote 28.

265. It is explained in *Sefer HaMaamarim 5659*, p. 415, and in *Sefer Ha-Maamarim 5711*, p. 209, that the body of Adam was susceptible to the sin of the Tree of Knowledge whereas after the Resurrection there will be no sin. Indeed, even in the Messianic era, bodies will be far more refined than they are now (see *Sefer HaMaamarim 5637*.)

Chapter 10

Life After the Resurrection

Will There
Be Eating
and Drinking?

Rav, one of the prominent Talmudic Sages, used to teach:[266] "[The World to Come will not be like this world.] In the World to Come, there will be no eating nor drinking nor procreation[267] nor business nor envy nor hatred nor competition; rather, the righteous will sit with their crowns on their heads[268] and delight in the radiance of the Divine Presence, as in the verse,[269] 'They beheld G-d, and they ate and drank.'" *(Rashi* understands this last phrase to mean that the Jews at Sinai were just as sated by

---

266. *Berachos* 17a. See *Reshimos,* Booklet #10, for further sources and discussion.

267. See *Sefer HaMaamarim 5679,* p. 414; *Likkutei Sichos,* Vol. XII, p. 178. See *Reshimos,* Booklet #10, p. 12, with reference to *mitzvos.*

268. In *Likkutei Torah — Derushim for Shemini Atzeres,* p. 89c, the Alter Rebbe writes in the name of *Ramaz* and R. Chaim Vital that the new souls to be revealed at the time of the Resurrection will serve as crowns for the *tzaddikim* who already have descended into the world.

269. *Shmos* 24:11.

the radiance of the Divine Presence as if they had eaten and drunk.*)*

Chapter 3 above has already discussed the difference in conception between *Rambam* and other thinkers as to the meaning of the "World to Come." According to *Rambam,* the above description refers to the presently-existing World of [disembodied] Souls, whereas in the future World of the Resurrection there will be eating and drinking and so on.[270] However, most authorities[271] hold that Rav is saying that after the Resurrection, though souls will then be reinvested in bodies, there will be no eating and drinking.[272]

In response to this majority opinion, *Rambam* argues[273] that it is absurd to consider that G-d would create a body equipped to perform physical functions such as digestion and reproduction in an era in which they will be extinct. One of the fundamental principles of the faith is that G-d does not create anything without a purpose. If there will be no need for physical functions, there will be no purpose for a physical body.

Ramban in *Shaar HaGemul*[274] refutes this argument at length. Firstly, there would be nothing novel in Rav's teaching if he was simply referring to the World of Souls. Moreover, after the Resurrection the body will attain the status of the

---

270. See *Rambam, Hilchos Teshuvah* 8:2, and the comments of *Raavad* and *Lechem Mishneh* there; *Sefer Chassidim,* sec. 1129; *Margaliyos HaYam,* sec. 19, on *Sanhedrin* 90b. See *Reshimos,* Booklet #10 (Shavuos, 5699; Paris), footnote 1.

271. See Rav Saadiah Gaon in *Emunos VeDeos,* end of sec. 47 and sec. 49; *Raavad* on *Rambam's Hilchos Teshuvah* 8:2; *Ramban,* at the end of *Shaar HeGemul;* Rabbeinu Meir ben Todros HaLevi in *Avodas Ha-Kodesh* 2:41; *Shelah,* in the introduction to *Beis David;* R. Shneur Zalman of Liadi in *Likkutei Torah, Parshas Tzav,* in the second of the *maamarim* beginning *Sheishes Yamim,* sec. 2 (p. 15c); *Likkutei Torah, Biur* on *Shuvah Yisrael,* p. 65d ff.

272. See *Maseches Kallah Rabbasi,* ch. 2.

273. *Iggeres Techiyas HaMeisim,* ch. 4.

274. P. 309 (Chavel edition).

soul, and will be sustained by spiritual sources rather than physical ones. This phenomenon is not new: Moshe Rabbeinu experienced it when he spent forty days and nights on Mt. Sinai.

The above view of *Ramban* is supported in the teachings of chassidic philosophy.[275] The Rebbe explains[276] that in this world body and soul are connected by means of food and drink, whereas in the World to Come, the body itself will derive sustenance from the light of the *Shechinah*. At the same time, this does not mean that there will be no eating or drinking. Rav's statement, that in the World to Come there will be no eating or drinking, means that eating and drinking will not then be necessary to keep soul and body together. However, there may be eating and drinking, though for a different purpose.[277]

The above explanation also resolves a seeming contradiction in the *Talmud*. On the one hand it is taught[278] that in the

---

275. *Likkutei Torah, Biur* on *Shuvah Yisrael*, p. 65d ff. See also: *Torah Or*, p. 20a; *Likkutei Torah, Parshas Emor*, p. 38c. Numerous sources in *Chassidus* explain that after the Resurrection the life-force of the body will be derived from a higher source than that of the soul; indeed, the soul itself will derive its sustenance from the body. See: *Sefer Ha-Maamarim 5637 (Hemshech VeKachah)*, sec. 91; *Sefer HaMaamarim 5666*, p. 528; *Sefer HaMaamarim — Kuntreisim*, Vol. II, p. 413b. See also: *Sefer HaMaamarim 5711*, p. 209; *Sefer HaMaamarim 5659*, p. 97; *Reshimos*, Booklet #10, p. 11.

   Speaking of the time of the Resurrection, the *Tzemach Tzedek* teaches that just as a man's hands will then be receptacles to the *Sefiros* of *Chessed* and *Gevurah*, and his head will serve as a receptacle to *Chabad* of the World of *Atzilus*, so too will his digestive organs "digest" the spiritual lights that are diffused from above, and will direct their effect to the lower worlds and kingdoms. (See *Or HaTorah — Devarim*, sec. 154, and *Shir HaShirim*, sec. 775-6.)

276. See *Shaarei Geulah*, p. 302, footnote 23.

277. See *Shaarei Geulah, loc. cit.*; *Likkutei Sichos*, Vol. XXI, p. 87. See also *Shaarei Halachah U'Minhag — Orach Chaim*, Vol. I, pp. 303-304, regarding the Third Meal of *Shabbos*, and ch. 12 below.

278. *Pesachim* 119b.

World to Come, G-d will prepare a festive meal for the righteous with the meat of the Leviathan, and most authorities
understand this not as a metaphor but as an actual feast.[279] If
so, does this not contradict the teaching of Rav with which this
chapter opened?

In an attempt to accommodate both positions, some
authorities maintain that this meal will take place in the Messianic era that *precedes* the Resurrection.[280] However, according
to those who maintain that it refers to the time of the Resurrection, how can there possibly be physical eating?[281] According to
the above explanation, however, although in the World to Come
eating will not be needed to fuse body and soul, it will still

---

279.   Rav Saadiah Gaon, as quoted in *Shvilei Emunah* 10:2; *Rashba* on
        Bava Batra 74b; *Ramban* on *Bereishis* 1:21; R. Bachye, *loc. cit.; Kad
        HaKemach*, end of sec. 8; *Raavan* in *Sefer Maamar HaSeichel; Ibn
        Ezra* on *Daniel* 12:2; *Raavad* on *Hilchos Teshuvah* 8:4; *Avodas Ha-
        Kodesh* 2:41; *Maharsha* on *Bava Basra* 74b; *Likkutei Torah, Parshas
        Tzav (loc. cit.).* In *Hilchos Teshuvah (loc. cit.), Rambam* implies that
        these words of the Sages are metaphorical, though without utterly
        excluding their simple meaning. And, indeed, *Ramban* (in his *Iggeres
        Hitznatzlus* on *Moreh Nevuchim*) states that it was heard explicitly
        from *Rambam* himself that the Sages are speaking of an actual meal
        with wine and the meat of the Leviathan. (This answers the objection
        of *Raavad.*) See also *Zohar* I, 135a.
280.   R. Avraham ben HaRambam in *Sefer Milchamos HaShem.*
281.   Some authorities (see *Rashba*, Rabbeinu Bachye and Ibn Ezra in pre-
        vious footnotes) maintain that the meal will take place at the very
        beginning of the period of the Resurrection. (This answers the com-
        ment of *Kessef Mishnah* on the *Raavad, Hilchos Teshuvah, loc. cit.*). In
        Likkutei Torah, however, it is implied that the feast will take place at
        the same time that the righteous sit with their crowns on their heads
        — and this is the very time of which Rav stated that there will be
        neither eating nor drinking. This seeming anomaly is resolved in *Sefer
        HaMaamarim 5666*, p. 105, which differentiates between two distinct
        periods within the era of the Resurrection. See *Likkutei Sichos*, Vol.
        XXI, p. 87.

remain a possibility — though for a different and higher purpose, such as the feast of the Leviathan.[282]

WILL THERE BE A DAY OF JUDGMENT AFTER THE RESURRECTION?

1. *Ramban*[283] answers Yes: on that Day every individual will be judged according to his deeds.

2. Abarbanel[284] argues that since everyone is judged after death, there is no reason for any additional judgment after the Resurrection. When the Sages speak of a Day of Judgment in time to come, i.e., after the Resurrection, they mean a day of punishment and revenge — but not of further judgment.

3. The *AriZal*[285] says that once a soul has already won atonement by experiencing Yom Kippur, and suffering, and reincarnation,[286] there is no reason that it should be judged further on a Day of Judgment. Rather, the classical references to the Day of Judgment speak of the judgment of the nations of the world.

---

282. In *Likkutei Sichos,* Vol. XV, p. 420, the Rebbe explains how the feast of the Leviathan signifies the revelation of the *rationale* underlying the Torah and the commandments; by contrast, the time in which there will be no eating signifies the future revelation of the Essence of Divinity by virtue of the unquestioning and *super*rational self-sacrifice of the Jewish people during the present era of exile.

283. *Sefer HaGemul.*

284. *Maayanei HaYeshuah* 8:7.

285. Quoted in *Nishmas Chaim* 1:17; see also *Midrash Talpiyos: Anaf Yom HaDin.*

286. One may ask: What about those who die so close to the time of Resurrection that they are not granted full atonement through reincarnation or suffering? The author of *Nishmas Chaim (loc. cit.)* writes that the punishment of these souls will be compressed into a short period so that they, too, will be granted entry to the World to Come.

Will Death
Survive the
Resurrection?

After the Resurrection, death will be no more.[287] Even
according to the literal understanding[288] of the verse,[289] "for [at
that time] the youngest will die a hundred years old," it does
not apply to the Jewish people, for whom death will no longer
exist. It refers to Noachides,[290] and even then, not to actual
death, but to death as a metaphor signifying a fall in the level
of one's spiritual attainment.[291]

---

287.   *Sanhedrin* 22a; *Zohar* I, 114a; *Derech Mitzvosecha* by the *Tzemach
       Tzedek*, p. 28. (For *Rambam's* view, see the beginning of ch. 3 above.)
288.   R. Chaninah in *Bereishis Rabbah* 26:2; see also *Pesachim* 68a and
       Sanhedrin 91b. In *Sefer HaMaamarim 5711,* p. 208, the Rebbe ap-
       plies this verse to the Messianic era.
289.   *Yeshayahu* 65:20.
290.   See *Sefer HaMaamarim — Melukat,* Vol. II, p. 280.
291.   *Likkutei Torah, Parshas Chukas,* p. 57a. See also: *Zohar* III, 135b,
       quoted in *Etz Chaim, Shaar* 9, ch. 2; *Mevo She'arim,* Vol. II, ch. 3.
          In a letter published in *Likkutei Sichos,* Vol. X, p. 211, the Rebbe
       applies this concept to the four levels of vitality within every Jew —
       (1) the divine soul, (2) the intelligent soul, (3) the animal soul, (4) the
       body — which correspond to the four realms of created matter: (1) the
       human, (2) the animal, (3) the vegetative, (4) the inanimate.
          If the divine soul falls to the point that it no longer yearns for Di-
       vinity, it is termed dead, and must be resuscitated by the study of
       Chassidus.
          If a person is young not only in years but also in intelligence, so
       that his intelligent soul, instead of controlling his animal soul, is
       drawn after its lively passions, this reverse in roles constitutes a fall in
       level and it is termed dead. Education *(chinuch)* restores it to its
       place.
          The animal soul, for its part, should at least live up to the standard
       of conduct maintained by animals, and not diverge from its appointed
       lifestyle. If, however, it transgresses the will of its Maker, it is in a
       state of death (for "the wicked during their lifetimes are called dead";
       Berachos 18b). This state, too, is reversible, for when rebuked and
       inspired to do *teshuvah,* the animal soul can again return to the obser-
       vance of *mitzvos.*

How Long
WILL THE
WORLD EXIST?

There is a well-known teaching of R. Katina,[292] "The world will exist for 6000 years and for/in one [thousand] will be destroyed, as it is written,[293] 'And G-d will be exalted alone on that day.'"

Some commentators suggest[294] that the destruction is literal: after 7000 years the universe will revert to its original state of nothingness. Others hold[295] that this is a reference to the era of Resurrection: the Evil Inclination will then be destroyed and removed from the world and there will be no more observance of the *mitzvos*. Still others[296] interpret the "one of destruction" as a reference to *one of* the six millennia. (If so, this could well be a reference to the millennium of upheaval in which we are living.) There is also a debate as to whether the *Halachah* confirms the statement of R. Katina[297] or not.[298] Indeed, the

---

The body serves as a receptacle to the soul. If it dies literally, the *chevrah kadisha* must then prepare it for eventual Resurrection.

292. *Sanhedrin* 97a. This teaching makes use of the phrase (in *Tehillim* 90:4) that likens a thousand years in G-d's sight to one passing day in the life of mortals.

293. *Yeshayahu* 2:11.

294. *Raavad* and *Kesef Mishneh* on *Hilchos Teshuvah* 3:8; *Kisvei HaRamban*, Vol. I, p. 188; *Ramban* and Rabbeinu Bachye on *Bereishis* 2:3; *Rama* in *Toras HaOlah*, Vol. II, ch. 25.

295. *Maggid Meisharim* by R. Yosef Caro on *Parshas Behar* and *Vayakhel;* Recanati on the Torah, *Parshas Behar*. In *Torah Or, Megillas Esther*, p. 96, the Alter Rebbe explains that destruction signifies that elevations have ceased.

296. Meiri, *Beis HaBechirah*, Introduction to *Avos*.

297. Responsa of *Rashba*, Vol. I, sec. 9. See also *Reshimos*, Booklet #7, p. 10.

298. *Moreh Nevuchim*, Vol. II, ch. 29; Abarbanel, *Mifalos Elokim* 7:3. In *Likkutei Sichos*, Vol. XXI, p. 453, the Rebbe points out that the statement of R. Katina is widely accepted as authoritative. Note also the discussion of the seven Sabbatical cycles (cited in *Sefer HaTemunah*)

Kabbalists speak of 50,000 Jubilee cycles through which the world will proceed in its process of elevation.[299]

---

that the world is to go through — but see *Torah Or, Parshas Shmos,* p. 51d. In *Shaarei Teshuvah,* p. 70b, the Mitteler Rebbe discusses the elevation of the soul in each of the 50,000 Jubilees of which the Sages speak. See also *Reshimos,* Vol. VII, p. 10.

299.   *Torah Or, Shaarei Teshuvah.*

CHAPTER 11

MITZVOS AFTER THE RESURRECTION

ETERNITY
OF TORAH
AND MITZVOS

After the Resurrection, will the 613 commandments still apply?[300] In particular, what of those that require involvement with the physical world? If, as some authorities hold,[301] there is no eating or drinking, how will one observe the *mitzvah* of reciting the Grace after Meals which is based on the verse,[302] "And you shall eat and be satisfied, and bless the L-rd your G-d"? More broadly, what is the meaning of the Talmudic

---

300. This chapter is based on a talk by the Rebbe that has appeared as an essay entitled *Kuntreis Mitzvos Beteilos LeAsid Lavo* ("An Essay on the Question of Whether the *Mitzvos* will be Abrogated in the Future," published in *Sefer HaSichos 5752;* Kehot, N.Y.). There are varying perspectives on this question, even within the *maamarim* of the Rebbeim of *Chabad.* For a full analysis of the relevant sources and views see: R. Yehudah Chayoun, *Otzros Acharis HaYamim,* ch. 12; and an essay by R. Yonasan Reinitz (in *Kovetz Shaarei Menachem,* Vol. II; New Haven, 5755), documenting all the sources in *Chassidus.*

301. See ch. 10 above.

302. *Devarim* 8:10.

teaching that[303] "the righteous will sit with their crowns on their heads and delight in the radiance of the Divine Presence"? And will there still be Torah study?[304]

This question in turn raises a more fundamental question — the eternal nature of the Torah. Were the commandments given to be observed only for a certain period, after which they would be revoked, or are they eternal?

Rambam writes:[305] "It is clear and explicit in the Torah, that the Torah is an eternal commandment; it is not subject to change nor subtraction nor addition." Elsewhere in *Mishneh Torah*[306] he clarifies this principle: "All the books of the prophets *(Nevi'im)* and all the Holy Writings *(Kesuvim)* will be dissolved in the days of *Mashiach*, except for the Book of Esther, which will remain — like the Five Books of the *Chumash* and like the legal rulings *(halachos)* of the Oral Law, which will never be revoked."

The idea that the books of the prophets will be dissolved in the Messianic era is based on a passage in the *Jerusalem Talmud.*[307] The reason given is that all the words of the prophets are intended either to reinforce adherence to the laws given through Moshe Rabbeinu in the *Chumash* or to admonish peo-

---

303. *Berachos* 17a.
304. See *Mabit, Beis Elokim — Shaar HaYesodos,* sec. 60.

> In an exposition of the verse from *Shema* (in *Devarim* 6:7) which commands us to constantly "speak of [the words of the Torah]," *HaYom Yom* (entry for 13 Menachem Av; cf. *Avos* 6:9) traces a man's involvement in Torah study through all the stages of his soul's life cycle. This involvement begins, even before the soul's descent to this world, with the time in which it is still in its original haven ("when you sit in your house"); it continues throughout his passage through life ("when you walk along the way") until the time of his passing ("when you lie down"); and it culminates at the time of his Resurrection ("when you rise").

305. *Hilchos Yesodei HaTorah* 9:1.
306. *Hilchos Megillah* 2:18.
307. *Megillah* 1:5; see also *Likkutei Sichos,* Vol. XIX, p. 177.

ple for negligence. (In the words of the last of the prophets, for example,[308] "Remember the Torah of Moshe, My servant.") In the Messianic era, when the law as given through Moshe Rabbeinu is fully observed, there is thus no more need for the words of the prophets. Furthermore, all the laws derived from the Prophets and the Writings are (previously) alluded to in the Five Books of the *Chumash* — and in the Messianic era, we shall be able to understand how to derive these laws directly from the *Chumash*.[309]

THE
ORAL
TRADITION

It is thus clear that all the exegesis and debate of the Oral Tradition will be abrogated and we shall be left with only the *halachos,* its clearly-defined laws. In the Messianic era, moreover, all the reasons for the commandments will be revealed. Indeed, our comprehension of the Torah will be on such a different level that when the prophet says that at that time[310] תורה מאתי תצא — "a Torah shall go forth from Me," the *Midrash*[311] extrapolates: תורה חדשה — "a *new* Torah shall go forth from Me" (or, in another version, חידוש תורה — "a *renewing* of the Torah shall go forth from Me"). Since the Torah is eternal, it is obvious that the *Midrash* is not speaking of a new set of laws; rather, it is speaking of the inner dimension of the Torah, the reasons and mysteries that will be revealed by *Mashiach.* Thus all that will remain from our pre-Messianic presentation of the Oral Tradition will be the actual laws, without the surrounding exegesis.

---

308.   *Malachi* 3:22.
309.   See *Mareh Panim* on the *Talmud Yerushalmi, Megillah* 1:5.
310.   *Yeshayahu* 51:4.
311.   *Vayikra Rabbah* 13:3, and commentary of *Radal* there.

This basic halachic framework of the Oral Law is foreshad-
owed in the *Mishneh Torah* of *Rambam*. As he writes in his
Introduction, "One may first read the Written Torah and then
read the present work and through it he may know the entire
Oral Torah, without needing to study any other intervening
work."[312]

At any rate, it is clear that *Rambam* rules that the Five
Books of Moshe and the *halachos* of the Oral tradition are eternal.

THE
MESSIANIC ERA
AND THE RESURRECTION

There is however an opinion in the *Talmud*[313] that the *mitzvos* will no longer apply after the Resurrection. According to
this opinion, the Messianic era will comprise two distinct periods. In the first period after *Mashiach* arrives, the whole of
Torah law will be in force and the *mitzvos* will be fully
observed. However, from the time of the Resurrection (which is
to take place forty years after the advent of *Mashiach*[314]), the
mitzvos will no longer be in force.

But what of the principle that all Torah laws are everlasting?

---

312.   Significantly, *Rambam* concludes his *Mishneh Torah* with the laws
       concerning *Mashiach (Hilchos Melachim,* chs. 11 and 12*),* for only in
       the Messianic era will all the laws of the Torah be in effect. Indeed,
       the Rebbe has said that the study of *Mishneh Torah* will hasten the
       approach of that era, for it is stated in *Vayikra Rabbah* 7:3 that the
       exiles will be gathered together in the merit of the study of *Mishnayos,*
       which the concise halachic rulings of *Mishneh Torah* strongly resem-
       ble.
313.   *Niddah* 61b. For a detailed presentation of sources, see: *Sdei Chemed
       — Klalim, Letter Mem,* sec. 218; *Divrei Chachamim,* sec. 53.
314.   See ch. 6 above.

In response to this apparent contradiction one could suggest that this means that they will last until the time of the Resurrection. In other words, the *mitzvos* apply only during the period of which it is written,[315] היום לעשותם — "[You shall observe the commandments... which I command you] *today, to do them.*" As the Sages explain,[316] the time to do the commandments is today, while in *this* world, but not "tomorrow, [when] you shall reap the reward," i.e., in the World to Come.[317] In this light, one may perceive the observance of the *mitzvos* as a means of refining and elevating the world, and once this has been achieved in the period of the Resurrection, they have no further function.[318]

MITZVOS
AS THE
WILL OF G-D

However, though *mitzvos* have an elevating capability,[319] the essence of a Divine command is the Divine Will — and this transcends time and place and even the world's spiritual level

---

315.   *Devarim* 7:11.

316.   *Eruvin* 22a; see also *Likkutei Sichos*, Vol. XXIX, p. 41.

317.   Observance of the *mitzvos* is mainly rewarded in the World to Come — the World of Resurrection. See: *Likkutei Torah, Parshas Tzav*, p. 15c, and *Shir HaShirim*, p. 65d; *Derech Mitzvosecha* by the *Tzemach Tzedek*, p. 14b. See also ch. 3 above.

318.   Cf. the teaching in *Bereishis Rabbah*, ch. 44: "The *mitzvos* were given only in order to refine creatures thereby." See also *Sefer HaIkkarim, Maamar Shlishi*, end of ch. 14.

319.   The Rebbe explains in a discussion of this subject that forms the basis of the present chapter, that the view of the *Midrash* and *Sefer HaIkkarim* (as in the preceding note) is the "external will of G-d," i.e., the will of G-d insofar as it is garbed in rational terms. However, His inner (i.e., essential and ultimate) will is independent of any world situation.

at any given moment.[320] The 613 commandments are a physical expression of the Will of the Divine Essence, which existed before the world was created and which will exist for all future time.[321] If so, how can we maintain that the *mitzvos* were intended to be valid only in this world, but not in the World to Come (the World of Resurrection)?

ONE PROBLEM RESOLVED, ONE PROBLEM POSED

A careful analysis of the context of the Talmudic teaching cited above[322] —that "the *mitzvos* will no longer apply in time to come [i.e., after the Resurrection]" — provides a solution to this apparently glaring contradiction.

The opinion is expressed that "a garment that includes *kilayim* [i.e., *shaatnez*, a prohibited mixture of wool and linen]... may be used for shrouds for the dead." This statement sparks off the following debate:

"Rav Yosef responded: 'This means that the *mitzvos* will no longer apply in time to come' [for otherwise, those resurrected would be wearing forbidden garments].

"Abbaye (some say it was Rav Dimi) objected: 'But R. Mani said in the name of R. Yannai that this permission applies only for the eulogy but not for the burial!'

---

320.   Herein lies the difference between the *mitzvos* given by the prophets and the *mitzvos* stated in the Torah. The former were momentary, because their purpose was only to ensure continued adherence to the Torah commands; the latter are eternal. See *Likkutei Sichos*, Vol. XIX, p. 182.

321.   For a full discussion of this point, see *Sefer HaMaamarim 5666* by the Rebbe Rashab of Lubavitch, p. 521, and also his *Toras Shalom*, p. 190.

322.   *Niddah* 61b.

"[Rav Yosef] replied: 'Was it not taught that R. Yochanan said that it applies even for the burial? And in this R. Yochanan is consistent with his own teachings, for R. Yochanan taught: What is meant by the verse,[323] "free among the dead"? — Once a man dies, he is free from fulfilling the *mitzvos.*'"

The commentaries find R. Yochanan's opinion problematic.

(1) The reason given — that the dead are free of *mitzvos* — is valid only when the departed are in the grave. Upon Resurrection, however, surely they would immediately transgress the prohibition of *kilayim.*

(2) Elsewhere[324] R. Yochanan says: "How is Resurrection deduced from the Torah?

"It is written,[325] 'Of [these tithes] you shall give G-d's heave-offering to Aharon the priest.' But would Aharon live forever?! After all, he did not enter the Land of Israel and thereby make it possible that *terumah* be given to him! Rather, this verse teaches that he will ultimately be resurrected, and the Jewish people will give him *terumah....*"

Now, if R. Yochanan holds that the *mitzvos* (such as *terumah*) will be observed after the Resurrection, how could he permit the use of *kilayim* for burial?[326]

---

323. Tehillim 88:6.
324. *Sanhedrin* 90b.
325. *Bamidbar* 18:28.
326. See *Sidrei Taharah* on *Niddah* 61b (except that this answer is valid only according to the textual reading of the *Rosh* who does not quote R. Yannai, whereas our text does).

    As a possible alternative answer, *Aruch LaNer* on this passage (based on *Yoma* 5b and the *Zohar* I, 40a) notes that Moshe and Aharon will be resurrected early, upon the arrival of *Mashiach.* Thus, in the first period of the Messianic era, when *mitzvos* will still be observed, *terumah* will be given to Aharon; later, after the universal Resurrection, when *mitzvos* will no longer apply, there will be no prohibition of *kilayim.* Accordingly, there is no contradiction between the

A Solution:
From Obedience
to Fusion

The Rebbe proposes the following answer:

In the above-quoted Talmudic discussion, the teaching of
R. Yochanan — that the dead are free of the commandments
— is cited as an explanation of Rav Yosef's view that there is
no observance of commandments after the Resurrection. However, though the dead are not obliged to observe *mitzvos*, the
mitzvos remain.

By way of clarification: A solitary entity may indeed possess a will, but this cannot be expressed as a commandment. A
commandment can exist only when there are two entities, the
Commander and the commanded, and the commandment connects the two.[327] Before the Resurrection, therefore, when man
and G-d are two separate entities, the notion of a commandment is conceivable. (Indeed, it is in the Messianic era, *before*
the Resurrection, that the commandments will be observed to
the ultimate degree.) After the Resurrection, when the entire
world will be permeated with the knowledge of G-d, man and
G-d will (so to speak) dissolve into one entity.[328] At that time a
mitzvah will not connect two separate entities; rather, it will
express G-d's unique Unity.

This conception enables us to resolve the seeming contradiction between the two teachings of R. Yochanan: on the one
hand, the use of *kilayim* for shrouds appeared to prove that
there will be no observance of *mitzvos* after the Resurrection,
and on the other hand, R. Yochanan's evidence for Resurrec-

---

two teachings of R. Yochanan. (See *Teshuvah MeAhavah,* Vol. III, p.
410.)

327. The very word *mitzvah* (מצוה — "commandment") shares a root with
      the Aramaic word *tzavsa* (צוותא — "together"). See *Likkutei Torah,
      Parshas Bechukosai,* pp. 45c, 47b.

328. *Zohar* III, 73a.

tion from the *mitzvah* of giving *terumah* appeared to prove the opposite.

In light of the above explanation, we can now understand that after the Resurrection the *mitzvos* will be observed not because they are commandments that connect two separate entities, the Commander and the commanded; rather, the entire creation will perform the will of G-d as a matter of course.[329] *Terumah* will automatically be given since it is the will of G-d. *Kilayim* may be used for shrouds since at the moment of Resurrection there will be no such prohibitive commandment; yet since it is the will of G-d that no *kilayim* be worn, the dead who will rise wearing *kilayim* will as a matter of course remove such garments upon their Resurrection.[330]

After the Resurrection, the relationship of Commander and commanded will make way for a world which is sensitive to the will of its Creator and responds to it spontaneously. In the same way, the link between *mitzvah* observance and reward and punishment will be severed. Instead, all of finite humanity will desire nothing more than to join hands in an ongoing quest for proximity with the Infinite Creator.

MITZVAH
AND
HALACHAH

We can now clearly distinguish between a *mitzvah* and a *halachah*. The *mitzvos* will no longer apply after the Resurrection; the *Halachah* is eternal. A *mitzvah* is a commandment

---

329. Cf. *Midrash Tehillim* on Psalm 73: "In time to come the very fig tree will cry out [to the intending transgressor], 'Today is *Shabbos!*'" See also: *Ramban* on *Devarim* 30:6; *Sefer HaMaamarim* of the Mitteler Rebbe — *Vayikra*, Vol. I, p. 433.

330. See *Maharatz* Chajes on *Niddah* 61b. One could further suggest that since it is the will of G-d that no *kilayim* be worn, by miraculous means those resurrected will not be wearing *kilayim*.

that connects; the *Halachah* is an expression of the Divine Will. The Divine Will is housed in the Torah, a "treasure" which existed before the world was created;[331] in the Torah G-d inscribed His very Essence.[332] It is thus eternal and independent of any and all considerations.[333]

TORAH
AND
MITZVOS

The above concept can also be expressed in a slightly different manner, using the terms Torah and *mitzvos*. *Mitzvos* are designed to enable the world to function in accordance with the Divine Will. The Torah *precedes* the world. Indeed, the world was created for the sake of the Torah,[334] so that the Divine Will expressed in the Torah which itself transcends the world, should also be expressed *within* the world. After the Resurrection, when the world will have been elevated, there will be no more observance of *mitzvos*, whereas the Divine Will as expressed in the *halachos* of the Torah is eternal.

We can now better understand the meaning of the above teaching of the Sages,[316] that the time to do the commandments is today, while in *this* world, but not "tomorrow, [when] you shall reap the reward," i.e., at the time of the Resurrection, in

---

331. *Shabbos* 88b.
332. *Ibid.* 105a.
333. Certain *halachos* relate to extremely improbable situations. Indeed, the *Gemara* itself *(Sanhedrin* 71a) testifies that the law concerning *ir hanidachas* (a city corrupted by idolatry) was never applied and never will be applied. As explained in *Tanya,* ch. 5, and *Tanya — Kuntreis Acharon,* p. 159b, the very existence of such laws demonstrates that the entire *Halachah* transcends worldly parameters: it is not just legislated in order to refine the world, but is simply an expression of the Divine Will.
334. *Rashi* on *Bereishis* 1:1.

the World to Come. For the true[335] "reward for a *mitzvah* is the *mitzvah* itself," i.e., the present connection with G-d that one achieves by its observance.[336] The true reward for the observance of *mitzvos* is to be elevated to the level of the Torah in the state in which it existed before Creation, a state in which the only entity really existing is a world that reflects the Will of G-d. This is the World of the Resurrection — a world which is truly connected and unified with G-d.[337]

BEIS HILLEL
AND
BEIS SHAMMAI

The above perspective also enables us to understand an otherwise perplexing teaching: Although nowadays (with a few exceptions) the law follows the view of the House of Hillel against the contrary view of the House of Shammai, in time to come the *Halachah* will accept the view of the House of

---

335. *Avos* 4:2.

336. See *Tanya*, ch. 39 (p. 104). See also footnote 327 above.

337. This perspective also explains a well-known exposition of the Sages on the non-literal level of *derush*. There is a verse that says *(Chavakuk 3:6)*, הליכות עולם לו *(halichos olam lo)* — lit., "the ways of the world are His." In the *Jerusalem Talmud (Megillah 1:5)*, these words are expounded as follows: "Do not read *halichos* ('the ways of the world') but *halachos* ('the laws of the Torah')." (See comments of *Korban HaEdah* and *Pnei Moshe* there.) There is a well-known principle (see *Likkutei Sichos*, Vol. XXI, p. 24) that "Do not read..." in the *Talmud* does not rule out the simple meaning of the verse being expounded: it adds to it. Both readings and both meanings are true. In our case, for example, we may understand that the *Halachah* comprises two elements: (a) *halichos* — "the ways of the world" which regulate the present conduct of the world according to the will of G-d (cf. *Rashi* on this verse); (b) *halachos* — "the laws of the Torah" insofar as they transcend the world. Before the Resurrection, therefore, the applicable reading is *halichos,* whereas in reference to the eternal nature of the law, i.e., after the Resurrection, the *Talmud* teaches, "Do not read *halichos* but *halachos.*"

Shammai as authoritative.[338] Would this switch of direction not appear to contradict the principle that the *halachos* are eternal and not subject to change?[339]

The *Mishnah* states:[340] "Any conflict of opinion that exists for the sake of heaven will survive... [such as] the conflict of opinion between Hillel and Shammai." As the Alter Rebbe explains,[341] the *Mishnah* means that both views are legitimate: in the present the *Halachah* follows the thinking of the House of Hillel and in time to come it will follow the thinking of the House of Shammai. In other words, the two views will (so to speak) take turns at being correct. The wording of the *Mishnah*, however, makes it clear that even when the law is changed so as to follow the House of Shammai, the difference of opinion will survive.

The Rebbe resolves this anomaly as follows. In the present era the *Halachah* follows the House of Hillel; when *Mashiach* comes the *Halachah* will follow the House of Shammai; at the time of the Resurrection, when the observance of *mitzvos* is suspended, only the *halachos* will remain — and then both views will be legitimate.

To explain: The views of the House of Hillel and the House of Shammai — so diametrically opposed that[342] "these permit and those prohibit" and[343] "the Torah resembled two Torahs"

---

338. *Mikdash Melech* on *Zohar* I, 17b, quoted in *Likkutei Torah, Parshas Korach,* p. 54c.

339. In the essay entitled *Torah Chadashah Me'iti Teitzei* (Kehot, N.Y., 5751), the Rebbe explains the halachic procedure by which this change will be effected: a majority of the Sanhedrin which will reconvene when *Mashiach* comes will decide in favor of the House of Shammai. The real issue, of course, is not one of technical procedure, but the question of which view will truly express the Divine will.

340. *Avos* 5:17.

341. In *Likkutei Torah, Parshas Korach,* p. 54b.

342. *Chagigah* 3b.

343. *Sanhedrin* 88b.

— are only opposed when the *Halachah* is translated into a commandment to be observed within mortal parameters. Within the finite confines of creation, only one of two opposing opinions can be "correct". In the here and now of this world, only one can be practiced: the other must be left waiting in the spiritual realm. In the present era, therefore, and so too in the Messianic era when *mitzvos* will still be observed, the *Halachah* must follow either one view or the other. At the time of the Resurrection, however, when G-d's infinity will be manifest, both views will be correct:[344] "Both these and those are the words of the Living G-d." Both opinions will then be relevant since G-d in His infinity can contain a contradiction.[345] This Divine capacity is echoed in the verse,[346] "G-d spoke one, and two I heard."

IN
CONCLUSION

The Messianic era will comprise two distinct periods.[347]

1. From the arrival of *Mashiach* until the Resurrection: During this period there will be no obstacles to the full obser-

---

344. *Eruvin* 13b.
345. See the Responsa of *Rashba*, Vol. I, sec. 418; *Sefer HaChakirah* by the *Tzemach Tzedek*, p. 34b.
346. *Tehillim* 62:12.
347. See *Likkutei Sichos*, Vol. XV, p. 417. In *Likkutei Sichos*, Vol. XV, pp. 563-4, the Rebbe compares (a) the tasks of the present era to the tasks of *baalei eisek* (those who are mainly occupied with the material workaday world, and whose prototype is Zevulun); (b) the tasks of the Messianic era to the tasks of *yoshvei ohel* (those who dwell in the tent of Torah study, and whose prototype is Yissachar); and (c) the era of the Resurrection to a perfect combination of divine service by body and soul together, as personified by Adam before the sin.

vance of the commandments. Indeed, their fulfillment in this world ("today — to do them") will be at its zenith.[348]

2. The period of the Resurrection: This is the time of reward for the observance of *mitzvos*. The ultimate reward will be the fusion of the Commander with the commanded, resulting in the suspension of the commandments. Instead of prohibitions and obligations, the world will be so filled with the knowledge of G-d that it will fulfill the Divine will spontaneously. This is the meaning of[303] "delighting in the radiance of the Divine Presence." At that time a *mitzvah* will not be perceived as a step towards a Divine reward: a *mitzvah* will be its own reward — the immersion of man in the Divine will.[349]

We opened this chapter with a simple question: If, as some authorities hold, there is no eating or drinking in the era of the Resurrection, how will one then observe the *mitzvah* of reciting the Grace after Meals?

---

348. Cf. ch. 3 above. See *Tanya — Iggeres HaKodesh,* Epistle 26. See, however, the Alter Rebbe's Note on *Tanya,* ch. 36, and *Likkutei Torah — Derushim* for Rosh HaShanah, p. 59c, which speak of *mitzvah* observance even after the Resurrection (as do the *Ran* and *Rashba,* quoted in *Sidrei Taharah* on *Niddah* 61b). See also *Shaar HaTeshuvah* by the Mitteler Rebbe, Vol. II, ch. 32. The above demarcation between the Messianic era and the era of the Resurrection solves many of the queries raised by the *Maharatz* Chajes (on *Niddah, loc. cit.*).

349. See, however, *Likkutei Sichos,* Vol. XIV, p. 182, and Vol. XV, p. 142, regarding the teaching in *Berachos* 64a: "*Talmidei chachamim* (Torah sages) have no rest in this world nor in the World to Come." There the Rebbe considers the time of the Resurrection itself as comprising an initial period of *mitzvah* observance to be followed by a period during which *mitzvos* will be suspended. (See *Sefer HaMaamarim 5666,* p. 97ff., and *Sefer HaMaamarim — Melukat,* Vol. II, p. 73, footnote 61.) The argument for *mitzvah* observance points out that Moshe and Aharon will offer sacrifices after their Resurrection. However, as mentioned above, *tzaddikim* will be resurrected during the Messianic era, before the general Resurrection. This matter requires further clarification.

The answer is that if a person were then to eat,[350] he would recite grace not in conscious fulfillment of a formal obligation, but as the spontaneous response of a created being who is utterly attuned to the Divine will. A more basic answer is that the question itself can only be asked so long as we perceive ourselves as being in the same frame of mind after the Resurrection as we are now — whereas in fact we will then all be as utterly immersed in the will of G-d as if immersed within the waters that cover the ocean bed.[351]

---

350. I.e., for the reasons discussed in ch. 10 above.
351. This closing phrase paraphrases the verse *(Yeshayahu* 11:9) with which *Rambam* chose to conclude the final chapter of his *Mishneh Torah* — possibly as an allusion to the state of Resurrection.

Chapter 12

Halachic Considerations

A
Blessing
to Recite

One of our daily expressions of praise is,[352] "Blessed are You... Who resurrects the dead." When the time comes, will the resurrected dead recite this blessing?

Let us consider comparable situations. Speaking of the Prophet Yechezkel's vision of the Valley of Dry Bones,[353] the *Talmud*[354] records varying views as to which song of praise was sung at that time. Speaking of the Binding of Yitzchak,[355] the *Midrash*[356] teaches that Yitzchak's soul flew from his body at the touch of the knife on his neck, and when his soul returned, he declared: "Blessed are You... Who resurrects the dead." The *Zohar*[357] teaches that at the time of the future Resurrection,

---

352. *Siddur Tehillat HaShem*, p. 52.
353. *Yechezkel* 37:1-15; see also ch. 14 below.
354. *Sanhedrin* 92b.
355. *Bereishis* 22:1-19.
356. *Pirkei deRabbi Eliezer*, sec. 31.
357. III, 267b.

the dead when revived will express their praise by singing,[358] "G-d, Who is like You?" Indeed, even when one sees a good friend after a mere 12-month interval, the *Talmud*[359] requires that one bless Him Who resurrects the dead.

Considering these sources, some halachic authorities hold that this blessing will indeed be recited at the time of the future Resurrection.[360]

PURIFICATION FROM RITUAL IMPURITY

The men of Alexandria once asked R. Yehoshua ben Chananyah...:[361] "Will the resurrected dead need to be sprinkled [with the purifying waters of the Red Heifer[362]] on the third and seventh day, or not?" He replied: "When they are resurrected we shall go into the matter." Others say [that he replied]: "When Moshe Rabbeinu[363] will come with them."[364]

The *Maharsha* paraphrases the above question as follows: Since many people were ritually unclean at the time of death, not having undergone purification when alive, will this state continue when they are resurrected? And he understands the reply of R. Yehoshua ben Chananyah to imply that once the

---

358. *Tehillim* 35:10; *Siddur Tehillat HaShem*, p. 168.
359. *Berachos* 58b.
360. See *Emunas HaTechiyah.*
361. *Niddah* 69b.
362. *Bamidbar* 19:1-22.
363. Cf. *Midrash Tanchuma, Parshas Chukas*, sec. 10; *Zohar* I, 113b; *ibid.* II, 157a; *ibid.* III, 168b.
364. For a detailed analysis of this passage see *Likkutei Sichos*, Vol. XVIII, p. 239-252; the Responsa entitled *Chasam Sofer* on *Yoreh Deah*, sec. 337. See, however, *Aruch LaNer; Aruch HaShulchan HeAsid, Hilchos Tumas HaMes* 9:5. See also *Or HaTorah* by the *Tzemach Tzedek* on *Bamidbar*, sec. 409 and 636-7.

original body has dissolved, no uncleanliness is transferred to the new body; hence no purification is required.

This discussion has wider implications. Anyone wishing to enter the courtyard of the *Beis HaMikdash* must be ritually clean. How, then, can *Mashiach* build the *Beis HaMikdash* and dedicate it if he is a person living today and has presumably come into contact with other people who are ritually unclean?

As one possible solution, one could rely on the principle that if the majority of the community is ritually impure, they are permitted to enter the *Beis HaMikdash* in order to conse-crate it. This was the case with the Hasmoneans in the Chanu-kah story.[365]

Alternatively, there is the opinion that Moshe and Aharon will be resurrected with the coming of *Mashiach,* and Aharon himself will sprinkle the waters of purification. This solution presupposes that a person who was ritually pure and then died and was later resurrected is not defiled by the transient state of death. (This assumption is explained by the above words of the *Maharsha,* that the resurrected body is not the same as the previous body.) However, what of those *tzaddikim* whose bodies do not decompose in the grave? Do their bodies not become ritually impure upon death? The *Halachah* establishes that the righteous upon death do not impart ritual impurity. Indeed, there are halachic authorities[366] who therefore allow *Kohanim* to pray at the graveside of great *tzaddikim.*

Others hold that the Prophet Eliyahu will sprinkle the cleansing waters, and that this is the meaning of the teaching in the *Talmud*[367] that "Resurrection comes through Eliyahu."[368]

---

365. See R. Sh. Y. Zevin, *HaMoadim BaHalachah* (in English: *The Festivals in Halachah,* Vol. II, p. 52).

366. See *Sdei Chemed; Aseifas Dinim, s.v. Eretz Yisrael; Shaarei Halachah U'Minhag* (pub. by Heichal Menachem), Vol. III, p. 395.

367. *Sotah* 49b (lower margin).

THE
STATUS OF
KOHANIM

Will those *Kohanim* who were anointed with olive oil in the times of the First *Beis HaMikdash*[369] require anointing afresh upon their Resurrection? Some sources state[370] that only Aharon and his sons will not require anointing. Others hold[371] that all *Kohanim* will have to be re-anointed since the body is new. By way of possible compromise, it has been suggested that the *tzaddikim* whose bodies did not decompose will not require anointing, whereas all other *Kohanim* will.

OUTSTANDING
SACRIFICES

Will a person who in his lifetime did not offer an obligatory sacrifice in expiation of his sin be required to discharge this obligation after Resurrection? The *AriZal* is evidently of the

---

368. The *Chasam Sofer* (in his *Chiddushim* on *Sotah* 49b) rejects the view that Eliyahu HaNavi will be ritually pure; rather, G-d Himself will cleanse us. The *Chida*, however, points out (in *Midbar Kdeimos, Maareches Alef*, sec. 26) that since the *AriZal* was cleansed by the waters of the *parah adumah* by Eliyahu HaNavi, this implies that the latter was ritually pure.

      The Rebbe explains (in *Sichos Kodesh 5720, erev* Shavuos, sec. 7) that "Resurrection comes through Eliyahu" because he refined his own materiality to such an extent that he entered heaven with his body: he transmuted it and permeated it with Divinity — and this, essentially, is the state of Resurrection.

369. *Rambam, Hilchos Klei HaMikdash* 1:7. (There was no sanctified oil in the Second *Beis HaMikdash;* see *Rambam, Hilchos Beis HaBechirah* 4:1.)

370. *Toras Kohanim, Parshas Tzav*, sec. 18; *Midrash Rabbah, Parshas Naso*, sec. 14.

371. *Rambam, Sefer HaMitzvos, Shoresh* 3; *Rashbatz* in *Zohar HaRakia*, quoted in the Responsa entitled *Rav Pe'alim*, Vol. II, *Sod Yesharim*, sec. 2; *Kli Chemdah* on the end of *Bereishis*.

opinion that the sacrifice must still be offered, but the question remains unresolved.[372]

Marriage
Forever

Will a man and his wife when newly resurrected need to be remarried, or does the original marriage bond continue? Some authorities suggest that a new marriage will have to be contracted.[373]

---

372.   See *Lev Chaim*, Vol. I, sec. 31; the *Chida* in *Pnei David* on *Parshas Vayikra*, quoting the *AriZal*; the Responsa entitled *Rav Pe'alim, loc. cit.* The *Chida* cites the *Gemara* (in *Yoma* 80a) as evidence that no sacrifice is required after death.

373.   See the *Ben Ish Chai* in the Responsa entitled *Rav Pe'alim, loc. cit.*
    The *poskim* debate the case of a person who died momentarily and was immediately resurrected (cf. the case cited in *Kesubbos* 62b, and the incident involving Rabbah and R. Zeira in *Megillah* 7b). See *Knesses HaGedolah*, cited in *Baer Heitev* on *Even HaEzer* 17:1; *Birkei Yosef* on the same source; *Siach HaSadeh*, Vol. II: *Likkutim*, sec. 4; the Responsa entitled *Chessed LeAvraham (Mahadura Tinyana)*, sec. 14; *Shoel U'Meishiv*, Vol. II, sec. 131; *Beis Yitzchak* on *Even HaEzer*, Vol. I, 6:14; *Avnei Nezer* on *Even HaEzer*, end of sec. 56.
    On the related question as to whether there will be procreation after the Resurrection, *Rambam* answers affirmatively (in *Iggeres Teiman*, cited in *Chiddushei Yad Rama* on *Sanhedrin*, beginning of *Perek Cheilek*). See, however, ch. 10 above.

A WOMAN
WITH
TWO HUSBANDS

A divorcee who remarries will remain married to her second husband upon Resurrection.[374] There is a difference of opinion as to the status of a widow who remarries.[375]

THE
HONOR DUE
TO PARENTS

Though the body dissolves and upon Resurrection is reconstituted, the obligation to honor one's parents will continue to apply.[376]

---

374. The Responsa entitled *Rav Pe'alim, loc. cit.; Anaf Yosef* on *Sanhedrin* (beginning of *Perek Cheilek*), in the name of *Sefer HaNitzachon; Yad Shaul* on *Yoreh Deah* 366:3.

375. The author of *Rav Pe'alim* holds that she will return to her first husband; the author of *Sefer HaNitzachon* holds that she will return to the second. The author of *Piskei Teshuvah* (sec. 124) first cites the reply of *Sefer HaTechiyah* of R. Saadiah Gaon — that this question will be resolved by Moshe Rabbeinu upon his resurrection — and then proceeds to cite the *Zohar* (I, 21b) as evidence that a woman in this situation will return to her first husband. (The question of where a remarried widow should be buried is discussed in *Gesher HaChaim,* Vol. I, ch. 27, sec. 7:3.)

376. The Responsa entitled *Rav Pe'alim, loc. cit.* See, however, *Toras Moshe* (by the *Chasam Sofer*) on *Shmos* 4:26.

CHAPTER 13

PRAYERS AND CUSTOMS

AT END OF
NIGHT, AT
END OF DEATH

Every morning, one's first wakeful words are *Modeh ani...*[377] — "I offer thanks to You, living and eternal King, for You have mercifully restored my soul within me; Your faithfulness is great." Some commentaries[378] on the *Siddur* perceive this statement as an affirmation of our faith in Resurrection: just as G-d returns our departed souls to our body anew each day, so too will He resurrect the dead.

Soon after *Modeh ani*, early in the Morning Blessings, comes the following explicit statement on the Resurrection:[377] "My G-d, the soul which You have placed within me is pure. You created it..., and You preserve it within me. You will eventually take it from me, and restore it within me in Time to Come. So long as the soul is within me, I offer thanks to You...,

---

377. *Siddur Tehillat HaShem*, p. 6.
378. *Anaf Yosef* in *Siddur Otzar HaTefillos*, based on *Bereishis Rabbah* 78:1 and *Eichah Rabbah* 3:21.

Master of all works, L-rd of all souls. Blessed are You, G-d, Who restores souls to dead bodies."

Likewise, three times a day, the second blessing of *Shemoneh Esreh*[379] praises Him Who "resurrects the dead with great mercy..., and fulfills his trust to those who sleep in the dust.... Who can be compared to You, King, Who brings death and restores life, and causes deliverance to spring forth! You are trustworthy to revive the dead. Blessed are You, G-d, Who revives the dead."[380]

THE
MELAVEH MALKAH
MEAL

With the *Melaveh Malkah* meal at the close of *Shabbos,* the Sabbath Queen is escorted on her way. This meal nourishes the *luz* bone, and from this bone the body will be reconstituted at the time of the Resurrection.[381]

---

379. *Siddur Tehillat HaShem,* p. 51.
380. In *Likkutei Sichos* (Vol. IV, p. 1081; Vol. VI, p. 84, footnote 29; and Vol. XIII, p. 75), the Rebbe discusses the connection between "great mercy" and the Resurrection.

 Sefer Chassidim (sec. 305) explains that the Resurrection is mentioned in *Shemoneh Esreh* immediately after the paragraph concerning the Patriarchs because one of the Biblical sources which the *Talmud* cites for the Resurrection relates to the Patriarchs *(Sanhedrin* 90b). (See *Torah Shleimah* on *Shmos* 6:4, and *Maharsha* on *Sanhedrin, loc. cit.)* In *Likkutei Sichos* (Vol. XXIV, p. 56, footnote 84), the Rebbe explains why G-d's power of giving rain *(gevuros geshamim)* is mentioned (by the phrase, *mashiv haruach umorid hageshem)* in the paragraph which speaks of the Resurrection. In *Derech Chaim* (p. 95), the Mitteler Rebbe explains how this power is related to the Divine attribute of *Gevurah.*
381. This is discussed in ch. 9 above. See the *Siddur* of R. Yaakov Emden, in the section entitled *Zemiros leMotzaei Shabbos, Mechitzah Daled; Kaf HaChaim, Hilchos Shabbos* 300:1; *Mishnah Berurah,* Vol. III, sec. 300:2, and *Shaar HaTziyun* there.

OUR BODY:
THE WORK OF
G-D'S HANDS

During the summer months between Pesach and Rosh Ha-Shanah it is customary to study a chapter of *Pirkei Avos* ("The Ethics of the Fathers") every *Shabbos* afternoon. Each week's reading is prefaced by the following *mishnah:*[382] "All Israel have a share in the World to Come, as it is said,[383] 'Your people are all righteous; they shall inherit the land forever; they are the branch of My planting, the work of My hands, in whom I take pride.'" This preface implies that knowing of the reward in the World to Come is a relevant introduction to the study of *Pirkei Avos.*

Now, the World to Come is the reward for a person's entire service of G-d through Torah and *mitzvos.* Why, then, was this particular *mishnah* selected as an introduction to *Pirkei Avos?*

The Rebbe Reb Heschel (in *Chanukas HaTorah: Likkutim,* sec. 209) observes that Adam introduced death into the world by eating of the Tree of Knowledge: those organs that were nourished at that time, which was a Friday, were destined to decompose. The *luz* bone alone will never decompose, because it is nourished only by the *Melaveh Malkah* meal.

The author of *Eliyah Rabbah* (on *Orach Chaim,* sec. 300) writes: "I have heard that the *luz* did not receive nourishment from the Tree of Knowledge." (The *Chasam Sofer* (Responsa on *Yoreh Deah,* sec. 337) writes similarly, without noting a source.) Surprisingly, however, *Eliyah Rabbah* also states (citing the *Levush,* and see also *Zohar* I, 137a) that "since the *luz* bone is not nourished by food, it did not benefit from the Tree of Knowledge." Above, however, we learned that the *luz* is nourished by the *Melaveh Malkah* meal. *Maavar Yabok* cites three opinions: (1) It receives no nourishment whatsoever from food; (2) it is sustained only by the food of *Shabbos;* (3) it is sustained only by the wine of *Havdalah.* In brief, the matter awaits clarification.

382. *Sanhedrin* 11:1.
383. *Yeshayahu* 60:21.

What specifically connects this reward with the content of *Avos*?[384]

To answer the above question a further introduction is necessary. One of the reasons given for studying *Avos* at this time of year is that man's desires are aroused at this time, and the study of *Avos* inspires him to pursue positive character traits.[385] The content of *Avos* is thus ethical.[386] However, the *Talmud* states[387] that the teachings of *Avos* are directed to a chassid, one who aspires to transcend the basic requirements of the law[388] — yet the custom is that every Jew, from the smallest who is just starting his spiritual path in life, to the greatest who is not distracted by bodily desires, both read *Avos*. This tractate thus possesses two dimensions — one ethical, relating to the control of one's passions, and so on, and the other chassidic, relating to the aspiration to transcend the letter of the law. Both these dimensions are represented in the preface, "All Israel have a share in the World to Come," as we shall now clarify.

The World to Come as mentioned in this *mishnah* is a reference to the Resurrection.[389] The reward of the Garden of Eden — the World of Souls — is not equal to all Israel,[390] whereas in the world of Resurrection, when all souls will be

---

384. This question in fact insists on being answered, for this tractate is beamed at a person who desires to be a chassid (see *Bava Kama* 30a) — and such a person will seek to serve G-d without an eye to reward.
385. See the Introduction to *Midrash Shmuel.*
386. See comment of *Bartenura* at the beginning of *Avos.*
387. Cf. footnote 384 above.
388. See *Derech Chaim* by the *Maharal.*
389. This was explained in ch. 3 above. Cf. *Bartenura* on *Sanhedrin* 11:1, and *Midrash Shmuel.*
390. In fact there are those who do not even merit the reward of the Garden of Eden: if not for the intercession of R. Meir, Acher would not have been admitted there *(Chagigah* 15b).

reembodied, all Israel will have an equal share, as is explained at length in the teachings of *Chassidus*.[391]

The reason for this distinction is that the reward of the Garden of Eden — for souls without bodies — is granted mainly for Torah study,[392] which varies (among other things) with the intellectual faculties of each individual soul. The reward of the Resurrection, by contrast, is granted for the *mitzvos* which were observed with and through the body; it is thus appropriate that it be granted to embodied souls.[393] Since individual Jews vary widely in their study of the Torah, their respective rewards in the Garden of Eden also vary widely. The observance of *mitzvos*, however, belongs to the realm of action, which is equal to all: even the sinners of Israel are as full of *mitzvos* as a pomegranate is filled with seeds.[394] For this reason, *all* Israel have a share in the Resurrection of the World to Come.

This raises a difficulty. How could it be that Resurrection, which is a greater reward than that of the Garden of Eden, is granted for the *mitzvah* observance of even a simple Jew? Surely the scholar's more elevated manner of serving G-d through Torah study should be more richly rewarded than the simple Jew's observance of the *mitzvos*.

The explanation: Superficially, all Jews are equal in the realm of action, which is the most basic of human faculties and

---

391. See the second *maamar* in the Appendix below. See also: *Torah Or, Parshas Yisro*, p. 73b; *Likkutei Torah, Parshas Shlach*, p. 46d; the *maamar* entitled *Ki Yish'alcha*, sec. 1, in *Sefer HaMaamarim 5679* and *Sefer HaMaamarim 5700*. See also *Sefer HaMaamarim 5672*, Vol. II, p. *alef*-112: Although the Resurrection will also comprise various levels, they are different from those of the Garden of Eden.

392. There is Torah learning in the Garden of Eden (see *Tanya*, ch. 41), but no observance of *mitzvos*.

393. See *Tanya* — *Iggeres HaKodesh*, ch. 17; *Derech Mitzvosecha, s.v. Tzitzis*, chs. 1 and 3.

394. *Chagigah* 27a.

requires neither mental nor emotive greatness. At the same time, this seemingly unimpressive faculty of *action* is uniquely precious.[395] G-d's ultimate will is that Jews should construct for Him an "abode in the lower worlds" — in this world, the lowest of all worlds.[396] It is specifically this World of Action that embodies the purpose of creation — the refining and elevation of the body and its environs. And since all Jews are "the branch of My planting and the work of My hands," all Jews feel this inner intent and carry it out.

We can now understand why the reward of Resurrection is granted specifically to *embodied* souls. G-d's intent of having an abode in this physical world is reflected in every Jew — who is one with the Essence of G-d — since G-d's choice focuses not only on the Jew's soul but also on his body.[397] This also explains the everlasting aspect of a Jew's physicality — the *luz* bone,[398] from which the body will be reconstituted at the time of the Resurrection. In this way, even when the physical world has been refined and elevated and transmuted into an abode for G-d, His choice of the Jewish body will still be manifest.

To revert to our original question: Why is the study of *Avos* prefaced by the *mishnah* that teaches that "All Israel have a share in the World to Come"? — In order to stress that the study of *Avos,* which guides one in refining the physical body, is vital to every Jew, for his body, too, is the work of G-d's hands.[399] It is in the work of His hands that G-d takes pride:[383]

---

395.   Cf. *Avos* 1:17: "What matters most is not study but action."
396.   *Tanya,* ch. 36.
397.   See *Tanya,* ch. 49, and at length in *Toras Shalom,* p. 120; see also *HaTamim,* Vol. I, p. 30.
398.   *Bereishis Rabbah* 28:3; *Zohar* I, 28b; *Tosafos* on *Bava Kama* 16b.
399.   The source of the phrase *yetzir kapai* ("the work of My hands") is *Pesikta Rabbasi,* sec. 47.

      The commentators on our *mishnah* ("All Israel...") note that it quotes the whole of the verse, including its final phrase ("the work of "though last in creation, it was first in [G-d's] thought."[400] Since it is the work of G-d's hands, every Jewish body has the potential to be refined.[401] Furthermore, since G-d[402] "devises means that he that is banished be not cast away from Him," even such a man will eventually be refined. Thus no one, however lowly he may be, has the right to excuse himself from refining his body.[403]

On the other hand, since G-d takes pride in the work of His hands, viz., the body, not even the man of stature described above by the Sages as a chassid, should underestimate the value of refining and elevating his body.

The lesson of the *mishnah* is therefore twofold: it reminds the individual tempted by his passions of the Divine Source of his body, and it teaches the chassid that even though he is beyond the temptations of the body he should not refrain from elevating the physical world, for in this lies the ultimate purpose of creation.[404]

My hands, in whom I take pride"), because it is this closing phrase that shows that the verse refers to the Resurrection of *embodied* souls. (Concerning the word "land", by contrast, it could be argued that it refers to the Garden of Eden; cf. *Likkutei Torah, Parshas Vaeschanan.*) This also explains why the *Rambam* (in *Hilchos Teshuvah* 3:5) does *not* quote the end of the verse, for according to his opinion the World to Come refers to the World of Souls.

400. From the *Lechah Dodi* hymn *(Siddur Tehillat HaShem,* p. 132). See also *Torah Or, Parshas Vayigash.*

401. Excepted are those who have no share in the World to Come; see ch. 5 above.

402. *II Shmuel* 14:14.

403. Cf. *Avos* 2:16.

404. *Likkutei Sichos,* Vol. XVII, p. 343.

THE
THIRD MEAL
OF SHABBOS

The usual custom of the Rebbeim of *Chabad* was not to eat bread for the Third Meal on *Shabbos* but to fulfill the *mitzvah* by partaking of lighter refreshments. The Rebbe fully explains[405] the basis for this custom both according to the *Halachah*, the legal framework of the Torah, and according to *Chassidus*, the inner dimension of the Torah; moreover, he explains how these two explanations obviously harmonize, since the revealed and the mystical dimensions of the Torah — the *nigleh* and the *nistar* — are (respectively) the Torah's body and soul.[406]

The Third Meal of *Shabbos* foreshadows the *Shabbos*-like state that will prevail in the World to Come. As to the well-known statement of the Sages[407] that "in the World to Come there is neither eating nor drinking...," the Rebbe points out that the world view of the *AriZal* and of *Chassidus* coincides not with the stance of *Rambam* — which identifies the World to Come with *Gan Eden*, and perceives the ultimate reward as being enjoyed by disembodied souls — but with the stance of *Ramban* and many other major authorities: The ultimate state and the ultimate reward at the time of the Resurrection will be enjoyed by souls that are garbed in bodies.[408] At that time the ultimate superiority of the body will finally become apparent.

In the above-quoted *sichah*, the Rebbe used these concepts and others to explain why the Third Meal should in fact be marked by eating, and also explains why alternatives to bread may be perceived as more than merely permissible substitutes.

---

405. See *Likkutei Sichos,* Vol. XXI, p. 84-88, and sources noted there.
406. *Zohar* III, 152a.
407. *Berachos* 17a.
408. See ch. 3 above, and sources there.

PREPARATION
FOR BURIAL:
BURIAL AS A
PREPARATION

Many of the laws and customs observed by the *chevrah kadisha* when preparing a man's physical remains for burial are inspired by the anticipation of Resurrection.[409]

For example: Though in practice the use of costly shrouds is forbidden, one of the Sages held that their use evidences a belief in the Resurrection.[410] Conversely, one of the reasons that cremation is forbidden is that it denies the principle of Resurrection.[411] Finally, an aerial view of a Jewish cemetery (known in the Holy Tongue as *Beis HaChaim* — "The Home of the Living") often discloses that the plots are arranged in such a way that the foot of each grave is directed towards the Holy Land; within Jerusalem, such as on the ancient Mount of Olives, towards the Temple Mount — so that the body of every departed Jew is laid to rest "as if ready to arise and go up to Jerusalem."[412]

---

409. *Emunas HaTechiyah,* ch. 4.
410. *Nimukei Yosef* to the *Rif, Moed Katan* 17a.
411. R. Yechiel Michl of Tukachinsky, *Gesher HaChaim,* Vol. I, pp. 155-6.
412. *Ibid.,* p. 138. (In some cemeteries, for the same reason, the custom is that the foot of each grave is directed toward the [path leading to the] gate through which one leaves.

CHAPTER 14

THE CONCEPT OF RESURRECTION IN AVODAS HASHEM

Throughout the literature of *Chassidus,* discussions of man's divine service are often enriched by a glance at the concept of Resurrection. Here is a brief sampling.

RESURRECTION: FROM CEREBRAL FRIGIDITY TO SPIRITUAL EMOTION

The Rebbe Rashab once taught:[413] "The *avodah* of serving G-d according to *Chassidus* comprises all possible levels.... The spiritual level represented by a corpse does not need much elaboration. At the same time, thank G-d, spiritual *avodah* also comprises a metaphorical revival of the dead. A corpse is cold — and there is nothing as frigid as natural intellect, mortal intellect. Accordingly, when one's natural intelligence compre-

---

413. *HaYom Yom,* entry for 11 Sivan.

hends a G-dly concept, and the spiritual emotions latent in the intellect [such as one's dormant love of G-d] are *enthused* and *moved* by this intellectual pleasure, that is a true revival of the dead."

RESURRECTION: BREATHING LIFE INTO PHYSICALITY

The Rebbe once explained:[414] All the rewards of the time to come are a direct result of one's present actions. Moreover, since[415] "the reward for a *mitzvah* is the *mitzvah*," every particular reward resembles its corresponding *avodah*. Thus, for example, the reward for the *mitzvah* of charity is wealth. Expounding on the non-literal level of *derush,* the Sages found a hint of this in the verse,[416] עשר תעשר (lit., "you shall surely tithe"). Noting the similarity between the root עשר ("to tithe") and the root עשר ("to grow rich"), the Sages teach,[417] עשר בשביל שתתעשר — "Tithe in order to grow rich."

At any rate, since every reward resembles its antecedent *avodah,* and since the ultimate future reward will be granted in the era of the Resurrection, it follows that even today there must be an element of Resurrection in our *avodah* that will be rewarded by Resurrection in the future.

This element of Resurrection may be sought in the following way. When a thinking Jew is involved in worldly things which are physical and moreover material, he realizes that they are not everlasting. Even a person who really desires any physical object realizes (even during the moments that he is enjoying it) that it does not last forever, and that there will

---

414.   At the *farbrengen* of *Yud* Shvat, 5723 [1963].
415.   *Avos* 4:2.
416.   *Devarim* 14:22.
417.   *Taanis* 9a.

come a time when even he himself will no longer enjoy it. It could take an hour, a month, a year, ten years, or even more — but at the end of the day he realizes that such pleasure is only momentary; such rewards do not last forever.

Contemplating this, he comes to understand that since the object of any physical desire is limited by time it cannot be termed true life or living.

A Jew's purpose is to inject an everlasting dimension into his physical life by connecting with G-d, Who in His infinity transcends time and place. When a Jew connects a physical object with G-d, he is in fact injecting it with real life and creating something that is everlasting.

Taking a dead object, i.e., something that is purely physical and limited by time and space, and infusing it with a breath of eternal life, — this is true Resurrection.

From this perspective we are able to appreciate the depth of a well-known teaching of the Sages:[418] "The righteous even after death are called alive...; the wicked even during their lifetime are considered dead." What does this mean? The wicked during their lifetime attach importance to the physical, which is limited and shortlived — in a word, dead. The righteous attach importance to the spiritual. They are thus alive even after death, since they charged their physical life with an eternal dimension.

A Jew's task is therefore to resurrect — to transform a fellow Jew who even during his lifetime is not alive into one of the righteous who even after death are alive.

---

418. *Berachos* 18a-b.

RESURRECTION:
REACHING OUT TO
A VALLEY OF DRY BONES

The following[419] is a condensation of a talk[420] in which the Rebbe drew lessons from one of the most dramatic narratives in all of the prophetic Books — the Prophet Yechezkel's vision of the Valley of Dry Bones.[421] This passage is read in the synagogue as the *Haftorah* for *Shabbos Chol HaMoed* Pesach.[422]

* * *

The Prophet relates his experience in these words:[423] "The hand of G-d was upon me, and He carried me out in the spirit of G-d, and He set me down in the midst of the valley, and it was full of bones. He made me pass by them around and around, and behold, there were very many over the surface of the valley, and behold, they were very dry. And He said to me: 'Son of man, can these bones come alive?' And I said: 'L-rd G-d, You know.' And He said to me: 'Prophesy concerning these bones, and say to them: O dry bones, listen to the word of G-d! Thus said the L-rd G-d to these bones: Behold, I will cause breath to enter into you, and you shall live; and I will lay sinews upon you, and bring flesh upon you, and cover you with skin, and put breath within you, and you shall live — and you shall know that I am G-d.'"

---

419.   Until the subheading, "Resurrection: Sharing Uninterrupted Life."

420.   On *Shabbos Parshas Acharei-Kedoshim,* 5746 [1986]. A complete translation of this talk has been published by Sichos In English as an essay entitled, "Dry Bones — Before and After." In *Reshimos,* Booklet #7, p. 10, the Rebbe explains why it was specifically Yechezkel who revived the Dry Bones.

421.   *Yechezkel* 37:1-15.

422.   *Tur Orach Chaim,* sec. 490, explains in the name of Rav Hai Gaon that this *Haftorah* is read during Pesach since the Resurrection will take place in the month of Nissan.

423.   *Yechezkel* 37:1-6.

Certainly the allegorical meaning of this experience was clear to the Prophet Yechezkel, and to all of his fellow exiles who sat by the waters of Babylon, and wept when they remembered Zion. Here was a clear assurance from G-d: He would gather together their stricken remnants, lead them home to *Eretz Yisrael,* and rebuild the *Beis HaMikdash* in Jerusalem.

Yet the vision yearns to utter more than a symbolic messages. As the words of G-d conveyed to us through His Prophets are eternal, this narrative must also speak to us today. And indeed, it is clearly a message addressed to Jews who are sensitive to the plight of those of their brethren who have lost the lifeblood of *Yiddishkeit,* the values and lifestyle of the Torah. It is a message that urges us to accelerate the vital work of spreading Torah and *Yiddishkeit* and disseminating the wellsprings of *Chassidus.*

There are those who argue that when Jews are on the outside, so to speak, spiritually no more than dry bones, there is no use speaking to them; one should wait until they have been brought within the fold, and have been clothed in flesh, sinews and a living spirit. Only then, so it is argued, can one teach these dry bones the word of G-d. There are even those who rationalize that publicly addressing these forgotten bones who lie forlorn on the valley floor is dangerously innovative. "We must walk in the footsteps of our revered predecessors," they argue; "why should we begin to deal with dry bones?"

The answer to these seekers of pious excuses is simple: The question of *which* footsteps of our predecessors are to be emulated, must be determined by consulting the Torah. And here, explicit before us in one of the 24 Books of the Written Torah, is the story of the Valley of Dry Bones. Precisely this is where to seek the real footsteps of our fathers that we should faithfully follow.

Yechezkel uttered his prophecies in the Diaspora. This particular prophecy was spoken in a valley, a place that is lowly and far away. The valley was filled with bones — of Jews who had not carried out G-d's will.[424] The bones were strewn about and forsaken; indeed, G-d Himself testified that they were very dry. Nevertheless, the Prophet Yechezkel tells us that G-d commanded him to speak to them: "And He said to me: 'Son of man..., prophesy concerning these bones, and say to them: O dry bones, listen to the word of G-d!'"

This is a lesson that must penetrate our hearts: If there are Jews who are void of the lifeblood and invigorating spirit of Judaism, who appear to be nothing more than dry bones, we must speak to them! For after all, they are[425] "children who have been taken captive among the gentiles." Their environments have deprived them of the means of discovering even the *alef-beis* of Judaism. Though in their present state they have neither spirit, nor sinews, neither nerves, nor flesh, nor skin, G-d tells us: Your heart has feelings, so awaken its innate sympathy for your Jewish brothers. You are a son of man, so imagine the pity your Father must feel for them. Go and tell those dry bones: "Listen to the word of G-d!" While they are still *in their present condition,* reach out and give them the word of G-d.

In response to this call, a person might limit himself to focusing his efforts on a single skeleton. Yechezkel therefore tells us that he was commanded to address a valley that was filled with bones. We must step out from our closed precincts into the center of town, into the streets of New York, and call out: "O dry bones, listen to the word of G-d!" We must not limit our outreach work to places in which there are more living, vibrant Jews than dry bones: we must address our message to all those vast valleys whose sole inhabitants are dry bones.

---

424.   *Sanhedrin* 92b and *Rashi* there.
425.   Cf. *Shabbos* 68b.

FORESTALLING
DANGER TO YOUR
NEIGHBOR'S LIFE

This duty is closely connected to another obligation:[426] "Do not stand still when your neighbor's life is in danger" (lit., "Do not stand still over your neighbor's blood"). To these words *Rashi* adds, "...witnessing his death when you are able to save him; for example, if he is drowning in a river or being attacked by a wild beast or robbers."

But these are not the only examples. When the Torah states that[427] "the blood is [associated with] the soul," it is telling us that a Jew's true lifeblood is his spiritual life, his Torah and *mitzvos.* The above verse — "Do not stand still over your neighbor's blood" — thus sounds a broader warning: Do not stand idly by if your neighbor is in spiritual danger. If his life-sustaining nutrients, his Torah and *mitzvos,* are ebbing away before your very eyes, you cannot look the other way. Instead of waiting until you are obliged to rejuvenate dry bones, step forward and reconnect his transfusion *before* he dehydrates.

Consider the first example that *Rashi* offers. Your neighbor may be drowning in a river of raging waters — a familiar chassidic metaphor for over-involvement in the turbulent torrents of materiality; he may be struggling to remain afloat in the surging ocean of his own corporeality. In such a situation the Torah admonishes us not to stand by idly: we can throw him a lifeline of Torah and *Yiddishkeit.* And if you ask, "Why me?" — the answer is that G-d would not show you such a phenomenon just to cause you sorrow: the very fact that Divine Providence ordained that you are there to see him drowning is itself proof enough that you can help him.

---

426.   *Vayikra* 19:16, and *Rashi* there.
427.   *Devarim* 12:23.

Obstacles
are Made
to Leap Over

The Rebbe Maharash used to say: "The world says that if
you can't crawl *under* an obstacle, then you have to clamber
over it. And *I* say: *Right from the outset, leap over it!*"[428]

This bold and optimistic approach to divine service disre-
gards conventional procedures and defies all inhibitions. It lifts
the individual into a higher realm in his own divine service and
streamlines his efforts at disseminating Torah and *Yiddishkeit*.

When one is confronted with the sight of a brother Jew who
is — spiritually speaking — in a life-threatening situation, the
appropriate response is to leap over all obstacles, without
fearing the (metaphorical) wild beasts or robbers. This is why
the above verse concludes, "I am G-d," for the ruler of all the
world's rivers and wild beasts and robbers is G-d Himself.
When a Jew sets out to save his fellow, he should fear nothing
on earth: G-d is by his side and will grant him success.

Outreach
is Not an
Optional Frill

There is another meaning to this concluding phrase, "I am
G-d." To these words *Rashi* adds, "...Who may be relied upon
to reward and to punish." When the Evil Inclination, whose
Yiddish nickname is *der kluginker* ("the sly fellow"), artfully
pours cold water on man's efforts, he needs to be reminded that
G-d grants reward. As we read in *Pirkei Avos*,[429] "Know... Who
your Employer is that will pay you the reward of your labor";

---

428. In the Heb./Yid. original the last sentence reads, *Lechat'chilah ariber!*
429. 2:14.

and again,[430] "Your Employer may be relied upon to pay you the reward for your labor."

Sometimes one needs to remind one's *Yetzer HaRa* of the punishment that awaits those who obstruct a Jew's divine service, who seek to sidetrack people who set out to save their fellow Jews by disseminating the knowledge and practice of *Yiddishkeit.* Among these people are the *shluchim,* the emissaries who carry out the holy mission of the Rebbe Rayatz by disseminating the wellsprings of *Chassidus* to the furthest outposts of Jewry. His agents (and[431] "an agent may in turn appoint an agent") should remember his directive: Disseminating *Yiddishkeit* is not a *hiddur mitzvah,* a spiritual luxury that technically may be dispensed with. It is quite literally a matter of life and death. As the Rebbe Rayatz declared: Do not stand still over your neighbor's blood; you can save him! And if you find him already in a state of dry bones, then bring him back to life!

Above all, if a formidable obstacle looms up on the horizon and threatens one's efforts at spreading *Yiddishkeit* and *Chassidus,* one should recall the motto of the Rebbe Maharash: "Right from the outset, leap over it!"

A PROMISE
OF
SUCCESS

In the prophecy of Yechezkel, G-d promises that such efforts will bear fruit, that they will bring dry bones back to life:[432] "Behold, I will cause breath to enter into you, and you shall live; and I will lay sinews upon you, and bring flesh upon you, and cover you with skin, and put breath within you, and you shall live — and you shall know that I am G-d.'"

---

430.   *Ibid.* 2:16.
431.   *Kiddushin* 41a.
432.   *Yechezkel* 37:5-6.

For indeed,[433] "I prophesied as I was commanded; ... and I looked, and behold, there were sinews upon them, and flesh came up, and skin covered them over,... and the breath of life came into them: they came alive and stood up on their feet, an exceedingly great multitude."

This passage gives us the potential and the guarantee — that when we carry out our mission by addressing the word of G-d to the dry bones all around us, through disseminating Torah and *Yiddishkeit* and *Chassidus,* we will succeed in bringing the dry bones back to life as "an exceedingly great multitude." Together with them we will greet *Mashiach,* for[434] "I will bring you to the Land of Israel... and I will place you in your land," and[435] "I will sprinkle upon you purifying waters." This task awaits *Mashiach* — may he come in our time!

May G-d bless all outreach projects with success. As to those whose missions take them to distant places, let them remember that as the physical distance [from here] is increased, the spiritual closeness is intensified. And carrying out the above-mentioned directives with *ahavas Yisrael,* with a sincere love of every fellow Jew as we are commanded in the Torah[436] — "Love your neighbor as yourself" — will bring about the revelation of G-d's innate love for every Jew. In this spirit of liberation may we go out to greet *Mashiach* with the true and complete Redemption, speedily in our days.

* * *

---

433.   *Ibid.* 7-8, 10.
434.   *Ibid.* 12, 14.
435.   *Yechezkel* 36:25.
436.   *Vayikra* 19:18.

RESURRECTION:
SHARING
UNINTERRUPTED LIFE

The Rebbe Rayatz once related:[437] "The Alter Rebbe was asked by his Rebbe, the Maggid of Mezritch, a question which he in turn had been asked by his Rebbe, the Baal Shem Tov: 'What do you remember?'

On this the Rebbe Rayatz commented: "This question has given life — a veritable Resurrection — to generations of chassidim. Resurrection means long life, true life. Death denotes interruption, whereas long life is life without interruption — and that is true life: no lack of life, but more than life. In *avodah* this means that not only is one alive, but one also animates others.

"In summary: True life is holiness, and holiness is infinite."

RESURRECTION:
THE ELEVATION
OF DIVINE SPARKS

In the primordial stages of creation, so the *Kabbalah* reveals, numerous sparks of Divinity fell as exiles into the realms of uncleanliness. There each spark is obliged to wait — until some individual somewhere chooses to make proper use of the particular fragment of materiality in which that dormant spark is embedded. By doing so he liberates and elevates it; he gives it renewed life.

---

437. *Sefer HaMaamarim 5710*, p. 262.

In the literature of *Chassidus*,[438] this animation of seemingly lifeless sparks is often termed resurrection.

RESURRECTION: REHABILITATION FROM SIN

Three times a day in the *Shemoneh Esreh* we say,[439] "Blessed are You, G-d, Who revives the dead." The Mitteler Rebbe explains[440] that this blessing refers not only to the ultimate Resurrection, but also to the present resurrection of those souls which, having sinned, now renew their connection with the G-d of Life through *teshuvah*. While in the state of sin they are termed "dead"; as the Sages teach,[441] "The wicked even during their lifetimes are called dead." When, however, they return in *teshuvah*, they come alive.

Every day, thanks to G-d's mercy, is a time for *teshuvah*; hence every single day comprises an element of Resurrection.

RESURRECTION: DEFYING THE INHIBITIONS OF NATURE

On the same day[442] on which the Rebbe delivered the above *sichah* on the vision of the Valley of Dry Bones, he opened a discussion of the Messianic era by quoting the words of *Rambam* at the conclusion of his *Mishneh Torah*:[443] "One should not entertain the notion that in the era of *Mashiach* any element of

---

438. See, for example, *Torah Or,* p. 9a, and *Torah Or* on *Megillas Esther,* p. 117c.
439. *Siddur Tehillat HaShem,* p. 52.
440. *Derech Chaim,* p. 95.
441. *Berachos* 18b.
442. *Shabbos Parshas Acharei,* 5746 [1986].
443. *Hilchos Melachim* 12:1-2.

the natural order will be nullified, or that there will be an innovation in the work of creation. Rather, the world will continue according to its pattern. Although Yeshayahu states,[444] 'The wolf shall dwell with the lamb...,' these [words] are an allegory and a riddle... Our Sages taught:[445] 'There will be no difference between the current age and the era of *Mashiach* except [our emancipation from] subjugation to the [gentile] kingdoms.'"

Now, is it not surprising that *Rambam* rules that in the Messianic era there will be no miracles? After all, one of the Thirteen Principles of Faith enunciated by *Rambam* himself is belief in the Resurrection, which is surely a major miracle.[446]

We may therefore assume[447] that there will be two periods within the Messianic era — an initial period that abides by the natural order, followed by a second period which will be miraculous. When *Rambam* quotes the statement in the *Gemara* that in the Messianic era there will be no deviation from the natural order, he is referring to the first period. Hence, even if there is no change at that time, as long as our people have been freed of foreign subjugation, the Messianic era has been ushered in. *Rambam* adds, however, that since no man knows exactly how all these events will unfold,[443] the possibility remains that miracles will occur immediately and the prophetic promise that "the wolf shall dwell with the lamb" is not a parable but literal.[448]

---

444. *Yeshayahu* 11:6.

445. *Berachos* 34b.

446. See also *Likkutei Sichos* for *Parshas Bechukosai*, 5745 [1985], sec. 9.

447. For a full discussion by the Rebbe on this subject, see *I Await His Coming Every Day* (prepared by Sichos In English; published by Kehot, N.Y., 1991), p. 51ff.

448. *Iggeres Techiyas HaMeisim*, ch. 6. See also *Likkutei Sichos*, Vol. XV, p. 417. According to this view, when *Rambam* in *Mishneh Torah* defines the Messianic era merely in terms of emancipation from foreign subjugation, he is only giving the minimum halachic criteria for that era; he is not ruling out the possibility of its being miraculous.

There will be no need to wait and see whether this first period will be miraculous or otherwise, for *Chassidus*[449] rules that the prophecy is literal and there will be immediate changes in the natural order.

The above explanation sheds light on the following anomaly. The *Haftorah* for *Shabbos Chol HaMoed* Pesach, in the middle of the festival, is the prophecy of Yechezkel[450] regarding the resurrection in the Valley of Dry Bones.[451] The *Haftorah* of *Acharon Shel* Pesach, the last day of the festival, is the prophecy of Yeshayahu[452] about the coming of *Mashiach*. Why is the expected order reversed?

The Alter Rebbe writes in *Tanya*[453] that the ultimate fulfillment of the purpose of creation — that G-d should have an abode in the lower worlds[454] — is attained by our current actions and spiritual labors. Our current actions should therefore foreshadow the Messianic state.

This kind of *avodah* is expressed in two ways:

(a) The thrust of every Jew's *avodah* is *geulah* — Redemption; its goal is to redeem the G-dly spark within himself and his surroundings.

(b) Every Jew's *avodah* should be steered by the attitude that there are no obstacles, which will indeed be the case in the Messianic era.

This second point carries extra weight if we realize that the Messianic era will be miraculous. This implies that our current

---

449.   See *Shaar HaEmunah* (end); *Or HaTorah — Nach* (Vol. III), p. 633b; *Sefer HaMaamarim 5637 [1877]*, chs. 17, 94.

450.   *Yechezkel*, ch. 37.

451.   The *Tur (Orach Chaim*, sec. 490*)* explains that since the ultimate Resurrection will take place in the month of Nissan, we read a *Haftorah* on a related subject on Pesach.

452.   *Yeshayahu* 10:32ff.

453.   Ch. 37.

454.   See chs. 2 and 3 above.

avodah toward bringing about the Messianic Redemption must also be pursued with supernatural strength.

This is the lesson we learn from the fact that the *Haftorah* of Resurrection precedes the *Haftorah* of Messianic Redemption: Our entire *avodah* toward bringing about the Redemption should be undertaken in a miraculous and supernatural matter. Rather than seeing obstacles, we should announce with[455] "words that come from the heart [and] enter the heart" that *Mashiach* is coming: the time of our Redemption has arrived.

IS
MY TIE
STRAIGHT?

One[456] of the Sages of the *Gemara* once declared to his disciples:[457] "The least among you can resurrect the dead."

It is well known how this statement applied to the disciples of the Alter Rebbe.[458] From this one may understand that when [a chassid] is at the level of a "disciple of Moshe" [i.e., standing in humble deference to his Rebbe], then even "the least among you [and with these words the Rebbe pointed at the chassidim whom he was then addressing] can resurrect the dead."

---

455.   *Sefer HaYashar* by Rabbeinu Tam, sec. 13; *Shelah*, p. 69a.

456.   This section summarizes a talk delivered by the Rebbe on *Shabbos Parshas Shemini*, 5748 [1988].

457.   *Avodah Zarah* 10b.

458.   The Rebbe Rayatz once said *(Sefer HaSichos 5703 [1943]):* "One may likewise apply this dictum to the disciples of R. Hillel [of Paritch — a renowned chassid]. Physical death is the absence of vitality, a state of frigidity. Spiritual death, too, is frigidity; one's prayers are cold; one's observance of the *mitzvos* is cold; even one's singing and dancing is cold. R. Hillel educated his students to have warm hearts; even the least sophisticated of them could resurrect — i.e., could warm up — their cold fellow Jews."

We are speaking not only of resurrection that relates to the spiritual *avodah* of oneself or of others; we are speaking even of the physical realm. There is a well-known story[459] that illustrates the teaching that one should "*think* good and things will *be* good": through positive thinking one can perform an act of resurrection. (In fact, "thinking good" not only transforms a

---

459.   Retold by the Rebbe Rayatz in *Likkutei Dibburim*, Vol. I, p. 317 (and in Eng. translation: Vol. II, p. 28):

One of the *mashpi'im* in the Tomchei Temimim Yeshivah was Reb Michael.[...] When he was a young man one of his children became so dangerously ill that his doctors said nothing could be done. He went straight off and told a group of his fellow chassidim of his grievous situation. They lent him strength, urged him not to despair because without a doubt the Almighty would be merciful, and advised him to set out at once for Lubavitch [to see the Rebbe Rashab].

Hearing this he broke out into tears. He would dearly love to go to Lubavitch, he said, but the doctors had said that now it was only a matter of hours; what was the point of setting out on such a journey?

One of the elder chassidim turned to him sternly: "Doesn't the *Gemara* tell us explicitly, אל ימנע עצמו מן הרחמים — 'Let no man preclude the possibility of mercy'? So for sure the advocating angels will persuade the Almighty to wait with His final decision until you reach the Rebbe!"

Reb Michael thereupon set out on foot for Lubavitch accompanied by a *chassidisher* friend, a tailor by trade, and once or twice they were able to shorten the journey by taking cheap rides with passing wagons. And as soon as they arrived there, Reb Michael had the good fortune to be admitted to *yechidus* at once.

"As I walked into the Rebbe's study," Reb Michael himself related, "and handed the Rebbe the *pidyon nefesh* with the child's name written on it, the thought flashed through my mind: 'Who knows what's doing with the child? Didn't the doctors say it was only a matter of a couple of hours?' And I wept bitterly.

"The Rebbe read the note and said: 'Don't cry. *Tracht gut — vet zain gut! Think* good and things will *be* good. Don't lament! You'll celebrate the *bar-mitzvahs* of your grandchildren.'

"Whenever hard times came," concluded Reb Michael — for in later years he was to suffer anguish in the upbringing of his children, "I would always picture to myself the Rebbe's holy face, and recall those holy words that he told me at *yechidus* — and things would work out well for me."

negative to a positive state: it even preempts the negative state before it occurs.)

And if there can be resurrection in the physical realm, how much more so in the spiritual realm, in which everyone has the ability to revive the "dead" in himself — for nothing can stand in the way of willpower.

Resurrection is called for not only when one has reached a situation comparable to death, but also, as the Sages say,[460] "One who falls in level is called dead." So, too, one whose level of *avodah* falls short of his full spiritual potential is also called "dead".

Consider the case of a certain individual who was born and raised among chassidim, who studied in the Tomchei Temimim Yeshivah, who was privileged to be given directives by the Rebbe [Rayatz], who used to deliver chassidic discourses, and so on — but who then made money and now argues that his mission in life is to be an industrious Zevulun,[461] a financial supporter of Torah institutions. If so, he argues, he no longer has the time to study *Chassidus* and "*daven* with *avodah*" (i.e., to meditate at length over the depths that *Chassidus* reveals in the prayers). Such an individual has fallen in level.

The same applies to a person who has remained a studious Yissachar[461] and has also taught many students, but who argues that he has no time for the self-refining labors of *avodah*. He, too, has fallen in level.

This applies especially to the exertion one invests in one's daily prayers. The Alter Rebbe rules in the *Shulchan Aruch* that before prayer one must reflect for an hour to concentrate one's thoughts. (As the *Mishnah* teaches,[462] "the early chassidim used to spend one hour" in preparation for prayer.) At the

---

460.   *Zohar* III, 135b; *Likkutei Sichos*, Vol. X, p. 211.
461.   See *Rashi* on *Devarim* 33:18.
462.   *Berachos* 5:1.

very least, one should pray in the manner described in *Kuntreis HaAvodah* and *Kuntreis HaTefillah.*[463]

One must ask oneself honestly: When was the last time one prayed with earnest preparation? I am not going to cause embarrassment by addressing this question to anyone personally — but everyone should look into the mirror (like those who religiously follow the local custom of checking their tie in the mirror before they go out) and realize whom the above words are aimed at.

---

463.   Essays on the chassidic way in prayer by the Rebbe Rashab. The latter has been published in Eng. translation (by Kehot, N.Y.) under the title, *Tract on Prayer.*

Appendix 1

"To Understand the Concept of Techiyas HaMeisim, The Resurrection of the Dead"

A Chassidic Discourse

The* *Mishnah* states:[1] "Every Jew has a share in the World to Come." In this *Mishnah*, the term "World to Come" refers[2] to

---

* This *maamar*, delivered by the Rebbe on *Shabbos Parshas Acharei*, 5746 [1986], was published to mark the conclusion of the eleven months during which the Rebbe recited *Kaddish* after the passing of his wife — the saintly *Rebbitzin* Chayah Mushka, of blessed memory — on 22 Shvat, 5788 [1988]. It was reprinted in *Sefer HaMaamarim — Melukat*, Vol. III, p. 33ff.

The above English version, footnotes included, is taken almost verbatim from *Anticipating the Redemption: Maamarim of the Lubavitcher Rebbe, Rabbi Menachem M. Schneerson, Concerning the Era of Redemption*, translated by R. Eliyahu Touger and R. Sholem Ber Wineberg (Sichos In English, N.Y., 1994), p. 15ff. The reader will note that this version intentionally reflects the distinctive flavor and style of presentation that characterizes all *maamarim*.

the "World of Resurrection." This is indicated by the continuation of the *Mishnah*: "The following do not have a portion in the World to Come: He who says that 'there is no indication in the Torah that the dead will be resurrected.'" The reason [why such an individual is denied a share in the World to Come] is, as the *Gemara* explains:[3] "He denied the Resurrection of the Dead, therefore he will not have a share in this Resurrection — measure for measure." Thus, [it is with regard to Resurrection of the Dead] that it is said: "Every Jew has a share in the World to Come."

Gan Eden, [the Garden of Eden, the spiritual realm of the souls,] {is at times also referred to as the World to Come.[4] Although *Gan Eden* exists now as well,[5] [it is given this name which implies a future event] because it is attained by man *after* his labor in this world[6]}. As the verse states,[7] "Who may ascend the mountain of G-d?... He who has clean hands and a pure heart."

Parentheses () indicate parentheses in the original Hebrew text; square brackets [] indicate additions made by the translators; squiggle brackets {} indicate square brackets in the original Hebrew text.

1. *Mishnah* (*Sanhedrin* 10:1), customarily recited before beginning the study of *Pirkei Avos*.

2. *Bartenura* (and other commentaries) on *Sanhedrin, loc. cit.; Midrash Shmuel*, beginning of *Pirkei Avos*.

3. *Sanhedrin* 90a.

4. *Rambam, Mishneh Torah, Hilchos Teshuvah* 8:8. Even according to the resolution in *Chassidus* (see *Likkutei Torah, Parshas Tzav*, p. 16c, *et al.*) that the World to Come (generally) refers to the Era of Resurrection, at times *Gan Eden* is also called the World to Come, as mentioned in the *maamar*, and annotated in footnote 11 below.

5. Accordingly, we can explain our Sages' rhetorical question, "Are there then three worlds?" (*Sanhedrin* 90b). Although it would seem that there are indeed three worlds: our world, *Gan Eden* and the Era of Resurrection (see *Sefer HaIkkarim*, ch. 30 and conclusion of ch. 31, quoted in *Or HaTorah, Parshas Shelach*, p. 543), since *Gan Eden* exists now as well, it may be considered as part of our world.

6. *Rambam, loc. cit.*

7. *Tehillim* 24:3-4.

This verse indicates that there many requirements for attaining the state of *Gan Eden*.[8] With regard to the Era of Resurrection (the principal appellation of the World to Come), by contrast, it is stated that "Every Jew has a share in the World to Come."[9]

This requires explanation. The revelations that will characterize the Era of Resurrection far surpass those of *Gan Eden*. This is evident from the fact that *Gan Eden* exists now as well, while the revelations of the Era of Resurrection will not be manifest until that time. Moreover, the revelation of the Era of Resurrection will follow (even) the Era of *Mashiach*.

{This is also indicated by the expression:[10] "There is none comparable to You... in this world; and none apart from You... in the life of the World to Come; there is nothing aside from You... in the Era of *Mashiach*; and there is none like You... in the Era of Resurrection of the Dead." These four epochs are arranged in ascending order. The revelation of the World to Come (in this context, *Gan Eden*[11]) is loftier than the revelation that can exist in this world. Higher still, is the revelation in the Era of *Mashiach*. And on an even higher plane is the revelation of the Resurrection of the Dead — superior even to the revelation in the Era of *Mashiach*.}

---

8. This applies to even the lower level of *Gan Eden*, as stated in the discourse *Ki Yishalcha* which is cited in the note that follows. See also the series of *maamarim 5672* [entitled *BeShaah SheHikdimu*], Vol. II, beginning of ch. 379 (foot of p. 779).

9. *Ki Yishalcha 5679* (*Sefer HaMaamarim 5679*, foot of p. 351ff.) and *Ki Yishalcha 5700* (*Sefer HaMaamarim 5700*, foot of p. 44ff.).

10. The *Shabbos* liturgy. See the detailed explanation of this concept in the discourse entitled *Ein Aroch Lecha 5652* (*Sefer HaMaamarim 5652*, p. 6ff.).

11. *Sefer HaMaamarim 5652, loc. cit.*; the series of *maamarim 5672* [entitled *BeShaah SheHikdimu*], Vol. I, ch. 279 (p. 565); II, ch. 380 (p. 781); III, p. 1387.

[This requires explanation.] Many conditions must be met
to merit the revelation of *Gan Eden*, while the revelation of the
Resurrection of the Dead, which is vastly superior to that of
Gan Eden, will be granted to *all* Jews.

II The core of one of the explanations offered with regard
to this matter is as follows: As stated in many discourses,[12] *Gan Eden* is granted as a reward for Torah study,
while the Resurrection of the Dead comes as a reward for the
observance of *mitzvos*. This explains why *Gan Eden* is a world
of (incorporate) souls, while in the Era of Resurrection, the
souls will be enclothed in bodies. For Torah study relates primarily to the soul, while the observance of *mitzvos* relates primarily to the body.[13]

All Jews observe *mitzvos;* indeed, "Even the sinners of
Israel are as full of *mitzvos* as a pomegranate [is full of]
seeds."[14] Therefore "Every Jew has a share in the World to
Come."

It is possible to explain that this is also the intent of the
Mishnah's citation of the prooftext,[15] "And your people are all
righteous; they shall inherit the land forever...." By quoting this
verse, the *Mishnah* not only testifies that all Jews have a share
in the World to Come, but also explains why this is so.

A person who observes *mitzvos* is referred to as "righteous",
a *tzaddik.* {Since all the *mitzvos* are referred to as *tzedakah*[16] —
"righteousness", those who perform *mitzvos* are termed *tzad-*

---

12. *Torah Or, Parshas Yisro,* p. 73b. See also *Sefer HaMitzvos* of the
    Tzemach. Tzedek, p. 15b; the discourses entitled *Ki Yishalcha 5679,*
    beginning of ch. 2 (*Sefer HaMaamarim, loc. cit.,* end of p. 353ff.), and
    5700, ch. 4 (*Sefer HaMaamarim, loc. cit.,* p. 48).
13. See *Tanya,* ch. 35 (foot of p. 44a ff.); *ibid.,* ch. 37 (p. 49a-b), *et al.*
14. *Eruvin* 19a; *Chagigah* 27a.
15. *Yeshayahu* 60:21.
16. See *Tanya,* ch. 37 (p. 48b). See also citations in *Sefer HaMaamarim
    — Melukat,* Vol. I, p. 308, footnote 33.

dikim — "righteous individuals"}.[17] Since "your people are all righteous," all Jews (even the sinners among them) observe *mitzvos*. Moreover, they are "filled with *mitzvos*"; i.e., the *mitzvos* they observe fill their entire existence and being. Therefore "they shall inherit the land forever" — the "Land of Life,"[18] which refers to life in the World to Come.

The above explanation, however, does not account for the *Mishnah's* mention of the conclusion of the verse, "they are the branch of My planting, the work of My hands, in which I take pride." [This phrase highlights] the essential virtue possessed by [all] Jews, that they are "the branch of My planting, the work of My hands" — (possessing this virtue independent of their observance of *mitzvos*).

[By quoting this phrase as part of the prooftext for the concept,] "Every Jew has a share in the World to Come," the *Mishnah* indicates that the share all Jews possess in the World to Come is (also) a result of their inherent virtue.

III [This leads to the conclusion] that there are two aspects to the revelation that will characterize the Era of Resurrection of the Dead:

(a) The reward for the observance of *mitzvos* ("your people are all righteous") — at that time, the Divine energy that is drawn down through the observance of the *mitzvos* in the present era will be revealed.

(b) (Afterwards,[19]) they will ascend to a higher level, the revelation of the inherent virtue in [every] Jew: [every Jew] is

---

17. *Likkutei Torah, Shir HaShirim*, p. 16c; the first discourse entitled *Kol Yisrael Yesh LaHem Cheilek LaOlam HaBa 5626* (*Sefer HaMaamarim 5626*, p. 192), *et al.*

18. *Or HaTorah — Nach*, on this verse in *Yeshayahu*, ch. 3 (p. 288).

19. After the revelation of the Divine energy the Jews draw down through the observance of *mitzvos* — see footnote 49 below — [they will merit the revelation of their essential virtue].

"the branch of My planting, the work of My hands, in which I take pride." This is an even higher level than [the revelation of] the Divine energy drawn down through the observance of *mitzvos*.

[This second aspect] represents the primary new dimension of the Resurrection of the Dead. For the revelation of the Divine energy drawn down through the observance of *mitzvos* will also exist during the Era of *Mashiach* (which will precede the Resurrection).

As explained in *Tanya*,[20] through our [positive] actions and Divine service at present, we draw the *Or Ein Sof* (G-d's infinite light) into our world. The revelation of this Divine energy will take place in the Era of *Mashiach* and in the Era of Resurrection. ([More particularly,] in the Era of Resurrection, this revelation will be on a higher plane.[21]) Thus the primary new dimension and the true ascent of the Era of Resurrection will be the revelation of the source of the Jewish people, the dimension which is rooted in G-d's very Essence.[22]

On this basis, we can explain the order of the verse: "Your people are all righteous" refers to the virtues achieved by the Jews through their divine service. As a result, "they shall inherit the land forever." Next comes the higher quality, "the branch of My planting...." It is possible to explain that after the Jews "inherit the land" and the Divine energy they drew down through their observance of the *mitzvos* ("Your people are all righteous") is revealed, their essential virtue as "the branch of My planting..." can then be expressed.

20. *Tanya*, ch. 37 (at the beginning and on p. 48a).
21. See *ibid.*, ch. 36, which mentions "the Era of *Mashiach* and *in particular,* when the dead will be resurrected."
22. See the series of discourses entitled *Yom Tov Shel Rosh HaShanah 5666*, p. 507, which states, "The ultimate ascent to be attained in the Future Era is that [the Jews] will reach their true root and source; there is nothing higher than this... [This relates to the expression] 'and there is none like You, our Deliverer in the Era of Resurrection of the Dead.' At that time, the true root and source of souls in the essential Truth of G-d's essence will be revealed."

We may say that the explanation found in many discourses (and mentioned above) — that the Divine energy that is drawn down through the observance of *mitzvos* will be revealed in the Era of Resurrection — [focuses on only one aspect of the Era of Resurrection]. [These discourses] speak of the reward that Jews will receive in the World to Come as a result of their Divine service in the observance of the Torah and its *mitzvos* in the present age.[23] The most complete form of reward [for this observance] is [the Torah and *mitzvos* themselves, i.e.,] — the Divine energy that the Jews draw forth through the observance of *mitzvos* will be revealed to them. [And this will be manifest in the Era of Resurrection.]

These discourses, therefore, [contrast this reward with] the reward received by the souls in *Gan Eden*, which is the comprehension of the G-dliness enclothed in the Torah that they studied in this world. The Torah is G-d's wisdom, the Divine illumination of *memale [kol almin*, G-d's immanent light, the G-dliness that enclothes itself in all the worlds, and relates to every particular level of existence*]*.

In the Era of Resurrection, [we will receive a more sublime] reward. Our eyes will behold the infinite Divine light[24] that is drawn down through the observance of the *mitzvos*, [the level of] Divine will (that transcends Divine wisdom). This refers to the light of *sovev [kol almin*, G-d's encompassing light which transcends the entire framework of limited existence*]*.

This reflects, however, only the reward received by the Jewish people for their divine service of observing the Torah

---

23. See *Ki Yishalcha 5700 (Sefer HaMaamarim 5700*, p. 45): "The similarity between them (*Gan Eden* and the Era of Resurrection) is ... they are *a reward* and *bestowal of goodness* [for one's actions in this world]."

24. The wording of the *Tzemach Tzedek* in the passage from *Sefer HaMitzvos* cited in footnote 12.

and its *mitzvos*.[25] The primary new dimension of the World to Come, however, is [a more elevated quality,] the revelation of the innate virtue of the Jewish people themselves — as "the branch of My planting, the work of My hands, in which I take pride."

IV Let us explain (the three levels, *Gan Eden* and the two levels that will be revealed in the Era of Resurrection) mentioned above. Our Sages teach:[26]

> The prophets all prophesied about the Era of *Mashiach* alone, but with regard to the World to Come, it is said, "No[27] eye has glimpsed it, but You alone."

Our Sages continue:

> What is [referred to by the verse]: 'No eye has glimpsed it'? This is *Eden*, upon which the eye of no created being has gazed. Should you ask: "Was not Adam, the first man, in *Gan Eden*, the Garden of Eden?"... [It can be explained that] the *Garden* is one entity [and there Adam was situated,] but *Eden* is yet another."

[This passage indicates that in] the World to Come, (the Resurrection of the Dead,) there will be a new dimension that surpasses [the revelation of] the Era of *Mashiach*. This will be the revelation of *Eden*, [a level so elevated, that until this revelation] "No eye has glimpsed it."

Although the World to Come will also include the revelation that is elicited through the observance of the *mitzvos*, this

---

25. The revelation of the *Or Ein Sof* drawn down by the Jewish people through their observance of the *mitzvos*, will be manifest within the world at large as well. {Nevertheless, the Jewish people will be privileged to a greater dimension of this revelation. See *Tanya*, conclusion of ch. 36 and ch. 37 (end of p. 47b ff.)}. [The fact that this revelation relates to the world at large] also indicates that this will not be the primary aspect of the World to Come.
26. *Berachos* 34b.
27. *Yeshayahu* 64:3.

is not the fundamental aspect of the World to Come. For this revelation will (in a general sense) also be appreciated in the Era of *Mashiach*. The fundamental element of the World to Come is the revelation of *Eden* — G-d's essential delight in the Jewish people, a delight that is even greater than the pleasure He derives from [their observance of] the Torah and its *mitzvos*.[28]

In many sources,[29] the difference between the Torah and its *mitzvos* is explained [as follows]. Within the Torah, which is G-d's Wisdom, is vested a radiation of G-d's delight. Within its *mitzvos*, which are G-d's will, is vested the essence of delight (which is called '*Eden*').

Thus with regard to *Gan Eden*, it is written,[30] "And a river went forth from *Eden* to irrigate the garden." This means that the delight that radiates to the souls in *Gan Eden* (as expressed in the comprehension of the Torah) is an effusion of *Eden*, [G-d's essential delight,] that has been severely contracted. [To speak in figurative terms,] it is drawn down through the river that separates the Garden from *Eden*.

The World to Come, however, in which the reward for the observance of the *mitzvos* is revealed, will include the revelation of *Eden* itself. [I.e., this passage appears to imply that the essential delight of *Eden* is the degree of delight attained through the observance of the *mitzvos*, and not the essential delight that G-d takes in the Jewish people *per se*, as explained above.]

---

28. See the series of discourses entitled *Yom Tov Shel Rosh HaShanah 5666*, p. 105. (P. 106) of that source states that it is possible to reach G-d's essential delight through *teshuvah* (repentance), but not through the observance of the Torah and its *mitzvos*. *Teshuvah* reveals the distinctive quality present within all Jewish souls, which is loftier than the Torah and its *mitzvos*.

29. *Sefer HaMitzvos*, cited in footnote 12.

30. *Bereishis* 2:10.

It is possible to offer [the following resolution]: In a general sense, [we can classify *Eden* as the essential delight in the *mitzvos*]. More specifically, however, the level of *Eden* that will be manifest in the World to Come is the revelation of G-d's essential delight in the Jewish people, a delight that surpasses His essential delight in the *mitzvos*.

This is evident from the fact that in the Era of *Mashiach*, there will also be the revelation of [His delight in] the *mitzvos* (in a general sense), and nevertheless [a distinction is made between the Era of *Mashiach* and the World to Come]. And it is emphasized that the revelation which "No eye has glimpsed," (the level of *Eden*,) will not be manifest in the Era of *Mashiach*. [Thus the fundamental aspect of *Eden* must be something other than His delight in *mitzvos*, and is defined as His essential delight in the Jewish people.]

V To clarify the superiority of the Era of Resurrection over the Era of *Mashiach* (and [in a more particular sense,] the difference between the two levels within the Era of Resurrection), it is necessary as a preface to explain the superiority of the Era of *Mashiach* over *Gan Eden*.[31]

The revelation of *Gan Eden* is granted to souls without bodies, while the revelation of the Era of *Mashiach* will be in our material world (as evidenced by the saying,[32] "The very land of Israel will produce wafers").

The reason for this difference is that within *Gan Eden* the Divine light which is revealed, the light of *memale [kol almin]*, is limited in nature. Hence, its revelation does not extend to the material plane. In the Era of *Mashiach*, by contrast, the infinite dimension of the *Or Ein Sof* will be revealed. Therefore, this revelation will encompass the material plane as well.

---

31.   With regard to the concepts which follow, see the series of *maamarim* *5672* [entitled *BeShaah SheHikdimu*], Vol. II, chs. 379-380 (p. 779ff.).
32.   *Shabbos* 30b, and sources cited there.

There is yet another difference [between the revelation of *Gan Eden* and the revelation of the Era of *Mashiach*. *Gan Eden* is characterized by a continual process of achievement, while the Era of *Mashiach* is characterized by rest.]

[To explain:] In general, *Gan Eden* is conceived of as being divided into two levels, the lower *Gan Eden* and the higher *Gan Eden*. Each one of these levels subdivides into an infinite number of strata.[33] As our Sages say,[34] "Torah scholars have no rest... 'they proceed from strength to strength,'"[35] [i.e.,] they constantly advance from level to level.

The phrase "they have no rest" implies that their elevation from level to level is attained through [effort and] spiritual service [as opposed to a state of "rest"].

To advance [to a higher rung in *Gan Eden*], the souls must first immerse in the River *Dinur*.[36] This immersion causes them to forget the comprehension [of G-dliness] and the [resulting] delight [which they experienced] on the lower level[37] [of *Gan Eden* and thus opens up their sensitivity to the higher level].

The actual advance [to the higher level] comes through the medium of the "pillar"[38] that exists between each level and the one above it. The pillar also nullifies the soul's previous degree

---

33.   *Iggeres HaKodesh*, Epistle 17.

34.   Conclusion of Tractate *Berachos*, and see additional sources cited there.

35.   *Tehillim* 84:8.

36.   [An Aramaic term meaning "river of fire." By immersing itself in this river, the soul burns away all vestiges of material consciousness.]

37.   *Zohar* I, 201a; II, 211b, 247a; Introduction to *Tikkunei Zohar* (p. 17a). See also *Torah Or, Parshas Mikeitz*, p. 31b, 32d, *Megillas Esther*, p. 96a; *Ki Yishalcha 5679*, ch. 1 (*Sefer HaMaamarim, op. cit.*, p. 352); *Ki Yishalcha 5700*, ch. 1 (*Sefer HaMaamarim, op. cit.*, p. 45). See also *Maamarei Admur HaEmtzai, Vayikra* II, pp. 821-822, and additional sources cited there.

38.   See *Zohar* I, 219a; II, 211a. See also *Maamarei Admur HaZakein, Parshiyos HaTorah* II, p. 773, and additional sources cited in the section of references (p. 984).

of comprehension. The difference [between immersion in the
River *Dinur* and elevation through the pillar] is, that the immersion in the River *Dinur* centers on the nullification of [the
comprehension experienced on] the lower level. The nullification achieved through the pillar, by contrast, comes as a result
of the revelation of the light that shines down from the higher
level.[39]

This is the intent of the statement that the elevation from
level to level [in *Gan Eden*] comes about through spiritual
service ("they have no rest"): i.e., the service of nullification.
Thus it resembles our divine service — *avodah* — in this
world.

The term *avodah* (עבודה) is related to the expression *ibud
oros* (עיבוד עורות) — "refining leather."[40] For our *avodah* is
intended for the purpose of "refining created beings"[41] and
bringing about self-nullification.

Our divine service on the earthly plane involves two
thrusts: "refraining from evil" and "doing good."[42] Similarly,
parallels can be seen with regard to the nullification involved
in ascending to a higher rung within *Gan Eden*: The nullification of the River *Dinur* resembles, as it were, refraining from
evil, and the nullification that results from the pillar, which, as
explained above, comes as a result of [the appreciation of] a
higher light, resembles our endeavors to do good.

This entire mode [of nullification and ascent] is relevant to
Gan Eden, but not to the revelations that will characterize the
Era of *Mashiach*. Although in that era there will also be con-

---

39.   See at length in the series of discourses entitled *Yom Tov Shel Rosh
      HaShanah 5666*, p. 15.
40.   *Torah Or, Parshas Mishpatim*, p. 76a. See *Likkutei Torah, Parshas
      Vayikra*, p. 2d, *et al.*
41.   *Bereishis Rabbah*, beginning of ch. 44, and additional sources cited
      there.
42.   [Cf. *Tehillim* 34:15.]

tinuous ascents, they will not involve going "from strength to strength"; i.e., there will be no need for a process of nullification and surging upward to ascend from a lower level to a higher level. Rather, the elevation to the higher level [will not require the nullification of the previous level. Instead,] as one exists on one's previous level, one will be able to comprehend a higher rung. (Additional explanation [of this concept] is, nevertheless, still required.)

VI To elaborate on this theme: [As mentioned above, the revelations of *Gan Eden* derive from the light of *memale kol almin,* G-d's immanent light, which enclothes itself within the various created beings.] The light of *memale* is drawn down to animate and bring into existence created beings through the pattern of *hishtalshelus;* [different levels of existence, one less refined than the other which are, like a chain, connected one to the other as] they extend downward.

First [this light is] vested in refined spiritual beings. Afterwards, it becomes vested in lower created beings, which [are inferior to the spiritual creations to the extent that their existence] can be described as an analogy to the higher form of existence. [I.e., just as an analogy uses an utterly different matter to illustrate the analogue, and yet the same pattern can be seen in both of them, so, too, the lower mode of existence is an entirely different form, but reflects the pattern of the higher mode.]

[This downward progression continues,] with the light being vested in even lower levels.[43] Thus the verse,[44] "He offered three thousand parables" [is interpreted to refer to three thousand levels of descent, i.e., from the highest realm in the

---

43. See at length in *Sefer HaMaamarim 5679,* p. 315ff., *et al.*
44. *I Melachim* 5:12. See also *Torah Or, Megillas Esther* 98b, *et al.*

world of *Beriah* to our material world,[45] each level appearing as a parable and an analogy to the level above it].

On this basis, it is possible to explain why the ascents within *Gan Eden* (which reflects the light of *memale kol almin* as mentioned above) from level to level require the nullification of the previous level [of consciousness]. [This represents the direct opposite of] the process of drawing down [the light of *memale kol almin*. For that process involves] enclothing the light in a series of garments, one less refined than the next. The process of ascent, by contrast, involves divesting these garments and nullifying the previous level.[46]

{On this basis, it is also possible to explain the statement mentioned in many discourses,[47] that even the souls of the Patriarchs and Moshe Rabbeinu, who have dwelled in the upper level of *Gan Eden* for more than three thousand years, will descend and again be enclothed in bodies [in the Era of Resurrection]. Since the revelation of the Era of Resurrection is vastly superior to the revelation of *Gan Eden* — even of [the most sublime levels] of the higher level of *Gan Eden* — [these souls will eagerly descend to receive this revelation].

The mention of "three thousand years" in the above expression parallels the "three thousand parables" mentioned previously and corresponds to the three worlds of *Beriah*, *Yetzirah* and *Asiyah*, for each world contains one thousand levels.

The statement "who have dwelled in the higher level of *Gan Eden* for more than three thousand years" implies that

---

45. [Each of the three worlds — *Beriah*, *Yetzirah* and *Asiyah* — can be described as having 1000 levels. For 1000 is ten cubed, a number resulting from the interrelation of the Ten *Sefiros*.]

46. See the series of discourses entitled *Yom Tov Shel Rosh HaShanah 5666*, *loc. cit.*

47. *Sefer HaMaamarim 5654*, p. 220; the series of *maamarim 5672* [entitled *BeShaah SheHikdimu*], *loc. cit.* (beginning of p. 780); *Sefer HaMaamarim — Kuntreisim*, Vol. II, p. 412a, *et al.*

during this period of time, these souls have divested themselves of all the garments (parables) of the three worlds of *Beriah*, *Yetzirah* and *Asiyah*. Thus, dwelling in *Gan Eden* for *more* than three thousand years means that [they have transcended these levels] and have even attained the state of *Atzilus*. Nevertheless, they too will descend into our material world and be clothed in bodies [at the time of the Resurrection]. For the revelation of the Resurrection will surpass that of *Gan Eden*, even the [higher] revelations of *Gan Eden* that come after [the light has been] divested of all its garments.}

[To summarize: an ascent to a higher level in *Gan Eden* requires that one first depart from his present spiritual station.] The ascent to a higher level [of consciousness] that will take place during the Era of *Mashiach*, by contrast, will not necessitate a departure from one's present level. [This will be possible, because at that time,] the *Or Ein Sof* which has no limits will be revealed. As such, the revelation will be manifest on the material plane as well.

VII Even the revelation of the Era of *Mashiach* will reflect [only] the light of *sovev kol almin*. Therefore, even in this era, there will be varying levels of revelation (as explained above). The revelation of the Resurrection, however, will (as a whole) be the same for all Jews.[48] For in the Era of Resurrection the essence of the *Or Ein Sof* that transcends [all possibilities of] division will be revealed.

There will be two aspects to this revelation:

(a) The revelation of the essence of the *Or Ein Sof* that [the Jewish people] will have drawn down through their observance

---

48. *Likkutei Torah, Parshas Shelach*, p. 46d; the series of *maamarim 5672* [entitled *BeShaah SheHikdimu*], Vol. II, p. 1, 112; see there.

of the *mitzvos*. This will raise the Jewish people themselves to a higher level.[49]

(b) The revelation of the innate [G-dliness] of the Jewish people, who are "the branch of My planting, the work of My hands, in which I take pride."

This quality of the Jewish people is even loftier than the revelation of G-dliness that they draw down through their study of the Torah and their observance of the *mitzvos*. For the source of Jewish souls is G-d's essence (higher than the source of the Torah and its *mitzvos*), and similarly, the Jewish body was chosen by G-d's essence.[50]

---

49.   To explain by referring to a *similar* concept. It is well known that [a soul] cannot attain the revelation of the Resurrection of the Dead without first receiving the revelation of *Gan Eden*. (See at length in the discourse entitled *HaYosheves BaGanim 5713*, ch. 8, in *Sefer Ha-Maamarim — Melukat,* Vol. II, p. 235). So, too, with regard to the revelation of the Resurrection of the Dead itself: First, there must be the revelation associated with the observance of the *mitzvos*. Afterwards, it is possible for the source of Jewish souls, inasmuch as they are rooted in G-d's essence, to be revealed.

50.   *Tanya*, ch. 49 (end of p. 69a ff.). See also *Toras Shalom*, p. 120.

Appendix 2

"All Israel Have a Share in the World to Come"

A Chassidic Discourse

In* the above-quoted *mishnah*,[1] the term "World to Come" refers to the Era of Resurrection,[2] as indicated by the con-

---

*   This *maamar*, delivered by the Rebbe on *Shabbos Parshas Acharei*, 5733 [1973], appears in *Sefer HaMaamarim — Melukat*, Vol. IV, p. 177ff.

   The above English version, footnotes included, is taken almost verbatim from *Anticipating the Redemption: Maamarim of the Lubavitcher Rebbe, Rabbi Menachem M. Schneerson, Concerning the Era of Redemption*, translated by R. Eliyahu Touger and R. Sholem Ber Wineberg (Sichos In English, N.Y., 1994), p. 40ff. The reader will note that this version intentionally reflects the distinctive flavor and style of presentation that characterizes all *maamarim*.

   Parentheses () indicate parentheses in the original Hebrew text; square brackets [] indicate additions made by the translators; squiggle brackets {} indicate square brackets in the original Hebrew text.

1.   *Sanhedrin* 10:1.

2.   *Bartenura* (and others) on *Sanhedrin, loc. cit.; Midrash Shmuel*, beginning of *Pirkei Avos*.

tinuation of the *mishnah* which states, "And the following do not have a share in the World to Come: He who denies that the concept of the resurrection has a source in the Torah."

Why is such a person not granted [a share in the World to Come]? Because, as the *Gemara* goes on to explain:[3] "He denied the Resurrection of the Dead, therefore he will not have a share in this Resurrection — measure for measure."

Thus [the Era of Resurrection] is the intent in the expression "Every Jew has a share in the World to Come." [Indeed, there is no alternative to this explanation. In other contexts, the term "the World to Come" is used to refer to] *Gan Eden*, [the Garden of Eden, the abode of the souls in the spiritual realms.[4] We cannot say that every Jew has a share in *Gan Eden*, for entry to *Gan Eden* is restricted,] as it is written,[5] "Who may ascend the mountain of G-d ...? He who has clean hands and a pure heart...." I.e., there are many requirements for entering *Gan Eden*, even the lower level of *Gan Eden*.[6] [No such restrictions apply regarding] the Era of Resurrection. [On the contrary,] "Every Jew has a share in the World to Come."[7]

This surely requires explanation, for the revelations that will characterize the Era of Resurrection will far surpass those

---

3.   *Sanhedrin* 90a.

4.   [Although the Garden of Eden refers to a physical place on this earth as reflected in the narrative of creation, the term is also used, in a figurative sense, to refer to the abode of incorporate souls in the spiritual realms.]

5.   *Tehillim* 24:3-4.

6.   See the discourse *Ki Yishalcha*, cited in the note that follows. See also the series of *maamarim 5672* [entitled *BeShaah SheHikdimu*], Vol. II, beginning of ch. 379 (foot of p. 779).

     Chagigah 15b states that were it not for the prayers of R. Meir, Acher would not have entered *Gan Eden* (i.e., even the lower level of *Gan Eden*).

7.   *Ki Yishalcha 5679 (Sefer HaMaamarim 5679*, foot of p. 351ff.) and *Ki Yishalcha 5700 (Sefer HaMaamarim 5700*, end of p. 44ff.).

of *Gan Eden.*[8] [This applies] even regarding the revelations within the higher level of *Gan Eden* — and indeed, those of the most sublime levels of *Gan Eden.*

{The concept [that the revelation that will characterize the Era of Resurrection is vastly superior to even the most lofty levels of *Gan Eden*] can be appreciated by the very fact that, at that time, all Jews will be resurrected. This will include even those souls that have been in *Gan Eden* for many thousands of years and which thrice daily are elevated to higher levels [of *Gan Eden*]. Nevertheless, they too will be clothed in bodies in the World to Come. [And they will eagerly desire to do so, because] the revelation that will characterize the Era of Resurrection is vastly superior to the revelation of even the most sublime level of *Gan Eden.*[9]}

[The question is thus reinforced]: Why is it that the lower rung, the level of *Gan Eden,* has many prerequisites which must be met if one is to merit its revelations, while the [far superior level, the] revelation of the Era of Resurrection, is the lot of all Jews?

II The above [question] can be resolved through a broader explanation of the concept that the revelation that will characterize the Era of Resurrection will far surpass the revelations of *Gan Eden.*

---

8. This follows the opinion of *Ramban,* conclusion of *Shaar HaGemul* (Edition Chavel, p. 309) [in contrast to the statements of *Rambam* in the *Mishneh Torah, Hilchos Teshuvah,* chs. 8, 9). *[Ramban's* opinion is echoed]* in the conclusive decision of *Chassidus.* See *Likkutei Torah, Parshas Tzav,* p. 15c, *Derushim leShabbos Shuvah,* p. 65d; *Sefer HaMitzvos* of the *Tzemach Tzedek, Mitzvas Tzitzis,* p. 14b; *Or HaTorah, Parshas Chukas* (foot of p. 809; *ibid.,* Vol. V, p. 1637). Significantly, in his discourses the Alter Rebbe mentions only the opinion of *Ramban.*

9. *Ki Yishalcha 5654 (Sefer HaMaamarim 5654,* p. 220); *BeShaah She-Hikdimu 5672, loc. cit.* (beginning of p. 780); *Sefer HaMaamarim — Kuntreisim,* Vol. II, p. 412a, *et al.*

Seemingly, [the opposite should be true]. *Gan Eden* refers
to the world of the souls (where the soul's perception is not
limited by a physical body). In the Era of Resurrection, by
contrast, the souls will [again] be clothed in bodies. Why then
will there be an even greater degree of revelation in the Era of
Resurrection, when souls will be clothed in bodies, than there
is in *Gan Eden?*

It is true that in the Era of Resurrection, the body will be
purified to the utmost, to the extent that it will resemble the
body of [the first man], *Adam HaRishon,* ([who was] formed[10] by
G-d's own hands)[11] [and whose refinement was so great] that
[he] "obscured the orb of the sun."[12] Indeed, in the Era of Resurrection, the body will attain a state of perfection greater even
than that of *Adam HaRishon.*[13]

[The extreme level of refinement that will characterize the
body] can explain why in the Era of Resurrection, the souls
vested in bodies will be fit vessels to receive a degree of revelation that is higher than the level which is presently received
by souls in an incorporate state [in the spiritual realms]. This,
however, does not explain why the revelation in the Era of
Resurrection will be appreciated by souls as they are clothed
within bodies. [Seemingly, since the body restricts the extent of
the revelation the soul can perceive, it would be preferable for

---

10. See *Bereishis Rabbah* 24:5; *Koheles Rabbah* 3:11 (2).
11. See at length in *Sefer HaMaamarim 5679*, p. 415; *Sefer HaMaamarim
    5711,* p. 209. [These sources explain] that since [in the Era of Resur-
    rection] the body will be formed by G-d through the "dew of resurrec-
    tion," the body will be on a level comparable to the body of *Adam
    HaRishon,* which was formed by G-d's own hands.
12. *Vayikra Rabbah* 20:2; conclusion of *Midrash Mishlei.* See also Intro-
    duction to *Tikkunei Zohar,* p. 10b. Examine also *Bava Basra* 58a.
        Sefer HaMaamarim 5679 and *5711, loc. cit.,* state: "His body was
    as refined and pure as light ... his body was like matter to form, i.e.,
    the soul, for they were comparable one to another."
13. See *Sefer HaMaamarim 5679* and *5711, loc. cit.*

the souls to receive these revelations without being encumbered by a body.]

Even in the Era of Resurrection, when the body will attain a state of absolute perfection, it will still be a physical body — and the inherent limitations of a physical entity are greater than those of a spiritual entity.[14] These include the limitations of time and space, characteristics that apply (primarily) to physical entities.[15] Nevertheless, in order for the soul to be able to receive the revelation of the Era of Resurrection, it must again be vested within a physical body.

[Indeed, there is a fundamental difference in the approach taken to receive the revelations of *Gan Eden* and the approach taken to receive the revelation that will characterize the Era of Resurrection]: In order to receive the revelations of *Gan Eden*, the soul must first divest itself of [all] material consciousness. [This implies a departure of the soul from the body, i.e., death. Afterwards,] the soul must immerse itself in the River *Dinur*,[16] in order that it be unable to recall any images of this world.[17]

---

14. Also noteworthy is the statement, cited above in footnote 12, that *Adam HaRishon's* body (and so, too, the body in the Era of Resurrection) was as "matter to form." We understand from this that even when the body is totally refined, "form" is still loftier than "matter".

15. Spiritual entities are also subject to [the limitations of] time and space [as these characteristics exist in a spiritual sense. These limitations, however,] stem from the fact that such entities can be considered as "physical" in comparison to absolute spirituality. Cf. *Tanya,* ch. 48 (p. 67b): "In spiritual matters, the characteristic of space is in no way applicable." And there the intent is space insofar as it exists in spiritual terms.

16. [An Aramaic term meaning "river of fire." By immersing itself in this river, the soul burns away all vestiges of material consciousness.]

17. *Zohar* I, 201a; *Ki Yishalcha 5679,* sec. 1 (*Sefer HaMaamarim, ibid.,* p. 352); *Ki Yishalcha 5700,* sec. 1 (*Sefer HaMaamarim, ibid.,* p. 45). See also *Lehavin Inyan Techiyas HaMeisim 5746,* sec. 5 (*Sefer Ha-Maamarim — Melukat,* Vol. III, p. 36) and the sources cited there. [See Appendix 1 above.]

{Similarly, in regard to the subsequent ascents [of the soul] within *Gan Eden* itself: As the soul ascends to a higher level, it must forget the [frame of] reference and the spiritual pleasure it experienced on the lower level.}[18]

[In contrast to this thrust to ascent,] an opposite movement is necessary [for the soul] to receive the revelation of the Era of Resurrection: [The soul descends and] enclothes itself within a physical body.

III [The above difficulties can be resolved by considering the following concept:] It is written,[19] "This is the Torah of man..."; i.e., the Torah resembles man. Just as man is a composite of body and soul, so, too, the Torah possesses [dimensions comparable to] a body and a soul.

In a general sense, this reflects the difference between the Torah and its *mitzvos:*[20] The 248 [positive] *mitzvos* are the 248 "limbs of the King,"[21] comparable [in analogy] to a person's limbs. The Torah, by contrast, can be compared to the blood, referred to as "the soul,"[22] [for it is the medium] that draws life into the limbs of [the body, i.e.,] the *mitzvos*.[23]

[The analogy between the *mitzvos* and a body can be taken further. Just as a body lives within a time and space continuum,] so too, [the observance of] the *mitzvos* is governed by time and space. There are designated times and places for their observance. The Torah, by contrast, transcends time and space.

---

18. *Ibid.*
19. *Bamidbar* 19:4. See also *Sefer HaMaamarim 5701*, p. 99.
20. *Sefer HaMaamarim 5701* (see also *Zohar* III, 152a) speaks of the body and soul of the Torah itself. [This does not contradict the concepts explained above.] For [the Torah and its *mitzvos*] are incorporated one within the other, therefore the Torah also possesses a body (as the *mitzvos* possess a soul — for the intent of the *mitzvos* is their soul).
21. See *Tikkunei Zohar, Tikkun* 30 (p. 74a), quoted in *Tanya*, ch. 4, and beginning of ch. 23.
22. *Devarim* 12:23.
23. *Likkutei Torah, Parshas Bamidbar*, p. 3a.

{Therefore, "A person who occupies himself in [studying] the laws of a burnt-offering is considered as if he had actually offered it."[24] This applies even when [he studies] at a time [inappropriate for bringing an offering] and in a place [where an offering] may not be sacrificed.}[25]

[Based on the above analogy, we can resolve the difficulty initially raised:] The body (and similarly, the *mitzvos*, which are compared to the body) are confined by the limits of time and space. The soul (and similarly, the Torah which is compared to the soul) are spiritual and transcend time and space.

A parallel to the relationship between the Torah and its *mitzvos* applies in relation to a person who studies Torah and performs *mitzvos:* Torah study involves primarily the soul, while the performance of *mitzvos* involves primarily the body.[26]

It is known[27] that the Torah's superiority over its *mitzvos* applies only as [these entities exist after being] drawn down into a revealed state [in our world]. In their source, however, *mitzvos* are on a superior level. For the Torah is the *wisdom* of G-d, blessed be He, while the *mitzvos* represent His *will,* and the level of will surpasses that of wisdom.[28]

Moreover, even after the Torah and its *mitzvos* are drawn down [into this world], the superiority of the *mitzvos* is readily apparent. For the Torah serves as an exposition and interpreta-

---

24. Conclusion of *Menachos; Shulchan Aruch Admur HaZakein, Mahadura Tinyana,* end of ch. 1; *Hilchos Talmud Torah* 2:11. See also *Likkutei Sichos,* Vol. XVIII, p. 413, footnote 25, and the addendum to that footnote.
25. *Likkutei Torah, loc. cit.*
26. See *Tanya,* ch. 35 (foot of p. 44a ff.); *ibid.,* ch. 37 (p. 49a-b), *et al.*
27. *Likkutei Torah, Parshas Acharei,* p. 28a, *et al.* Note that *Likkutei Torah,* on p. 26d ff., speaks of the superior quality of the Torah in relation to its *mitzvos* (quoting the passage of *Likkutei Torah* cited in footnote 21). Nevertheless, even this text (p. 28a) states that *mitzvos* are rooted in a higher source.
28. *Sefer HaMitzvos* of the *Tzemach Tzedek,* p. 15b, *et al.*

tion of the *mitzvos*.[29] [This implies that there is a superior quality to the *mitzvos* that the Torah can merely explain.]

We can appreciate that similar concepts apply with regard
to the soul and body of man {which resemble the Torah and its
mitzvos}: Although the body receives its vitality from the soul,
the source of the body is superior to the source of the soul.

{[These concepts are reflected in the relationship between
G-d and the Jewish people:] As explained in other sources,[30]
G-d's loving connection with the souls of the Jewish people
resembles a natural love, as it were, akin to a father's love for
his child. It is in this vein that it is written,[31] "You are children
unto G-d, your L-rd." [Although this reflects a very lofty form
of love, even this love has its limitations.] It is rooted in a level
[within G-dliness] where the import of [the souls], the objects
of [G-d's] love, is recognized. [Since there is an external source
— the souls' positive virtues — which motivates this love,] it
does not emanate from His essence itself.

G-d's loving connection with the bodies of the Jewish people, by contrast, does not stem (from [an appreciation of] the
inherent virtue of their bodies. Nor does this choice reflect [the
relationship between a father and] his child, who share a fundamental connection. Instead, [this love] comes about because
G-d chooses the Jewish body.[32] And this choice is entirely free,
[with no restrictions upon it, and no rationale which compels
it].[33] [Such a preference has only one possible source,] His very
essence.}

---

29. *Likkutei Torah, Parshas Acharei, loc. cit.*, p. 26d.
30. See *Sefer HaMaamarim — Melukat*, Vol. III, p. 276.
31. *Devarim* 14:1. See the beginning of ch. 2 of *Tanya*, which explains
      that this refers to the soul's relationship with G-d.
32. *Tanya*, ch. 49 (end of p. 69a ff.). See also *Toras Shalom*, p. 120.
33. [The intent is that G-d's essential love for the bodies of the Jewish
      people does not result from an awareness of their positive qualities.
      Were that to be the case, the love would be only as strong as the Jews'

This explains why the soul, [a refined spiritual entity,] can be drawn down to animate the body. Since the body is superior to the soul in its source, [it has the power to motivate the soul to descend and grant it life].

(Following a similar motif, we find the Torah explains and expounds the *mitzvos*. [As explained above, it directs its focus in this direction], because the source of the *mitzvos* is superior to that of the Torah).

IV There is [another] difference between the Torah and its *mitzvos* [which is relevant in this context]: All Jews are equally obligated in the observance of the *mitzvos*. In regard to Torah study, by contrast, there are a multitude of categories: [At one end of the spectrum are] those whose sole occupation is the study of the Torah. There are those who have the opportunity, and who are hence obligated, to actually "toil in Torah study during the day and at night."[34] [At the other end of the spectrum are] people who are occupied in commerce who may discharge their obligation by studying "one chapter [of the Torah] in the morning and one chapter in the evening."[35]

The reason for this difference is explained as follows:[36] *Mitzvos* are G-d's will (as stated above), and [the quality of] will defies division. The Torah, by contrast, is Divine wisdom, and wisdom is subject to diversity.[37]

---

virtues. Rather, His love for us comes as a result of His choice, a factor that transcends the entire range of human virtue (or its absence).]

34.   *Yehoshua* 1:8.

35.   *Menachos* 99b; *Hilchos Talmud Torah* of the Alter Rebbe, 3:4.

36.   The series of *maamarim* 5672 [entitled *BeShaah SheHikdimu*], Vol. I, ch. 4 (p. 8), ch. 52 (p. 93).

37.   [The intent is that will is undefined. When a person wants something, his attention is not directed to the entity insofar as it exists within its own context, but insofar as it is the focus of his desires. Intellect, of which wisdom is the first quality, by contrast has as its goal the comprehension of an entity as it is. This necessitates the appreciation of the various qualities the entity possesses.]

This motif can also be applied with regard to actual Torah study and performance of *mitzvos*. The *mitzvos* are performed by all Jews: "Even the sinners among Israel are as filled with *mitzvos* as a pomegranate [is filled with seeds]."[38] This is not the case with regard to Torah study.

[The rationale for this concept can be explained as follows:] It is only on an overt level[39] that some measure of fault may be found in a Jew; [in essence, all Jews are fundamentally good. Accordingly, with regard to Torah study, which relates primarily to the Jews' souls, at a level of revelation, the possibility for inadequacy exists. In regard to the performance of *mitzvos*, by contrast,] since *mitzvos* express G-d's will and relate to the [Jew's] body which was chosen by G-d's essence, they are of universal relevance [and are observed] by all Jews.

V This, then,[40] is the meaning of the teaching, "Every Jew has a share in the World to Come." Although the revelations in the World to Come (the Era of Resurrection) are vastly superior to the revelations of *Gan Eden*, nevertheless, this [loftier degree of] revelation will be [accessible] to all Jews.

By way of explanation: [The revelations of] *Gan Eden* reflect [merely] the Torah that one has studied in this world. The revelation in the World to Come, by contrast, will be the result of the *mitzvos* that are presently performed. Since, as explained

---

38. Conclusion of *Chagigah*.
39. The soul is also rooted in G-d's essence. Nevertheless, it is possible to say that since G-d's love for the Jews' [souls] is similar to a natural love (as explained earlier in the text), therefore, when compared to G-d's essential choice [to love and to be connected to] the bodies of the Jewish people, [His relation to our souls] reflects an aspect of revelation [and not essence]. This subject still requires further explanation.
40. With regard to the subjects to be explained see also the *maamar* entitled *Lehavin Inyan Techiyas HaMeisim 5746*, cited in footnote 17 above, sec. 2, and the sources cited there. (See Appendix 1 above.)

previously, the observance of *mitzvos* relates to all Jews, "*Every Jew has a share in the World to Come.*"

This [also] explains why the revelations of the Era of Resurrection will be appreciated by souls as they are clothed within bodies. For the performance of *mitzvos* is primarily related to the body, as explained above.

[The fact that the revelations of the Era of Resurrection will relate primarily to our bodies, for they are associated with the actual observance of the *mitzvos,* does not exclude our souls. On the contrary,] it is possible to explain that the revelations of the Era of Resurrection will be appreciated by the souls as well (as they vest themselves within bodies).

To cite a parallel concept: Our Sages state, "Great is Torah study, for it leads to action."[41] The fact that Torah study leads to action amplifies the greatness of the study itself. {[This relates to a concept] explained in the series of discourses [entitled *Yom Tov Shel Rosh HaShanah*] 5666:[42] When a person's Torah study is directed to discovering a ruling pertaining to the actual performance of a *mitzvah,* he will toil to a greater extent. Accordingly, he will obtain a deeper understanding of the Torah concepts he is studying.}

[To apply this concept to the analogue: Since the soul's Torah study leads to the body's performance of *mitzvos,* the soul will also enjoy the benefits that will be appreciated by the body — the revelation of the World to Come.]

Similarly, the Torah of the World to Come, the Torah of *Mashiach,* will be characterized by two dimensions: The Torah in and of itself will reach a level of completeness. In addition, we will appreciate the superior quality of Torah that results from its connection to the *mitzvos.*

---

41.   *Kiddushin* 40b; *Bava Kama* 17a.
42.   P. 390ff.

[A similar concept applies in regard to the soul in the Era of Resurrection.] At that time, the source of all the souls will be revealed. In addition, the soul will also be granted the revelation that is associated with the body ([and that results from] G-d's essential choice of the body).

May it be G-d's will, that as a result of our deeds and divine service, especially through the service of "spreading forth your wellsprings outward,"[43] we will be privileged to study the Torah of *Mashiach*, from the mouth of *Mashiach*, in the immediate future.

---

43.   As stated in the famous letter of the Baal Shem Tov, printed at the beginning of *Keser Shem Tov*, the spreading of the wellsprings of *Chassidus* precipitates "the coming of the master" — the King *Mashiach*.

Other Recent Titles Issued by S.I.E. Publications

Proceeding Together, the early talks of the Rebbe, in 1950 (1995)

Sichos In English, selected talks 1978-92, free translations, 51 vols.

In the Garden of the Torah, insights in the weekly Torah Readings, 2 vols. (1994-95)

Timeless Patterns in Time, Chassidic Insights into the Cycle of the Jewish Year, 2 vols. (1993-94)

In the Paths of Our Fathers, insights in the Ethics of the Fathers (1994)

A Partner in the Dynamic of Creation, on womanhood (1995)

Basi LeGani, Yud Shvat 5711 (1951), first chassidic discourse delivered by the Rebbe (1990)

Sefer HaMinhagim, Chabad-Lubavitch Customs (1992)

To Know and to Care, contemporary chassidic stories about the Rebbe (1993)

Please Tell Me What the Rebbe Said, Torah insights for children, 2 vols. (1993-95)

At Our Rebbe's Seder Table, commentary and stories (1995)

From Exile to Redemption, chassidic teachings on the future Redemption and *Mashiach* (1992)

I Await His Coming Every Day, analytical studies of Maimonides' rulings on *Mashiach* and the Redemption (1991)

Sound the Great Shofar, essays on the imminence of the Redemption (1992)

Seek Out the Welfare of Jerusalem, analytical studies of Maimonides' rulings concerning the construction and design of the Holy Temple (1994)

Anticipating the Redemption, chassidic discourses of the Lubavitcher Rebbe concerning the era of Redemption (1994)

מוקדש

לחיזוק ההתקשרות לנשיאנו

כ״ק אדמו״ר זי״ע

◆

נדפס ע״י

הרה״ת ר׳ יוסף יצחק הכהן וזוגתו מרת שטערנא מרים

בניהם ובנותיהם

שרה רבקה ובעלה הרה״ת שמעי׳ שי׳ קרינסקי

ובתם ריזל

מרדכי זאב הכהן, זלמן שמעון הכהן,

חי׳ שצערא, איסר אשר הכהן, זהבה, חנה,

ישראל הכהן, רפאל הכהן וריזל

שיחיו לאורך ימים ושנים טובות

גוטניק